THE *Perfect* Country Garden

THE *Perfect* Country Garden

Sunniva Harte

Trafalgar Square Publishing

*In memory of my Grandmother,
for whom all plants grew
and all birds sang.*

First published in the United States of America in 1997 by
Trafalgar Square Publishing,
North Pomfret, Vermont 05053

Printed in Singapore

Text copyright © 1997 Sunniva Harte
Design and layout copyright © 1997 Conran Octopus Limited

Commissioning editor Stuart Cooper
Project editors Tessa Clayton, Helen Ridge
Copy editor Claire Calman
Editorial assistant Tanya Robinson

Art editor Sue Storey

Picture research Julia Pashley

Production Mano Mylvaganam

ISBN 1–57076–097–7

Library of Congress Catalog Card Number: 97–60166

CONTENTS

INTRODUCTION

A SCENTED ROSE TUMBLING from a mellow brick archway; a ramshackle shed, half-hidden by ivy and honeysuckle; long grass laced with wildflowers – who could resist the quiet joys of a perfect country garden? The appeal of such a garden lies not in sophistication or grandeur, but in its simplicity and apparently artless charm. An informal collection of familiar and useful plants and plain ornaments, enclosed within lichen-encrusted walls, can speak to the heart much more directly than a row of imposing statues or a display of horticultural brilliance. Unforced grace and style hold sway, and rules are set aside more often than they are followed, to give the country garden its characteristic unfettered beauty.

LEFT *This cottage is almost obscured from view by this sea of familiar country garden flowers. Soft pinks and blues weave in and out of each other, while magenta-colored foxgloves and white campanulas bring emphasis and height to the scheme.*
ABOVE *A heavily scented, old-fashioned rose is ideally placed by a window; on still evenings its heady perfume will pervade the room within.*

A sense of belonging

More than any other type of garden, the country garden has a strong sense of belonging to its natural setting. Local materials and vernacular styles are used for garden structures, walls, and detailing, serving to root the garden in its location. They also provide a sense of continuity, a link with tradition. Many of the plants in the garden are local, too, or have become native in the fields and woodlands around, like the billowing grasses in a backyard in Virginia, which bring the meadow into the garden. The landscape is often one of the most glorious features of the country garden, defining its entire mood, whether it is a farmhouse set amid lavender fields in Provence, a thatched cottage in rural Britain, or a clearing in the wilds of New England. Many country gardens use their surroundings as an extension of the garden, "borrowing" views and external features as part of their inspiration and character. By creating gaps in hedges or using open fences or low walls at their boundaries, you make mature trees, open vistas, distant mountains, lakes, rolling pastures or picturesque buildings an intrinsic part of the garden.

FAR LEFT Senecio aureus, *or squaw-weed, with its sunshine-yellow flowers, grows lushly beside a dark, tranquil pool. The appeal of such a wild garden lies in the harmonious blend of native plants, which are woven together in such a way that the scene appears to be entirely natural.*

LEFT *A mountain house is surrounded by a garden filled with colorful plants that cope well with the extreme weather conditions. Yellow Jerusalem sage is a fitting companion for the taller broom, while roses thrive in the fresh mountain air above clumps of salvias and irises. A rough, narrow, grass path weaves its way among the flowers, emulating a mountain track.*

Working with nature

The best country gardens are in harmony with nature as well as with their surroundings. Whether they are exposed to coastal winds, dry Mediterranean summers, or the extremes of a continental climate, wise country gardeners learned long ago not to pit their strength against the elements but to garden with nature and grow only what would thrive in the given conditions. Nature is the controlling force in the country garden, blurring distinctions between the natural and the man-made: flower seeds are blown into the crevices of walls and joints in paths, while wooden and metal structures and stone ornaments are weathered and worn to become natural features.

ABOVE *Were it not for the simple wooden fence, it would be difficult to tell where this garden ended and the field beyond began.*

RIGHT *Unsophisticated rustic seats complement the roughly growing areas of this garden perfectly. The weather is no enemy of such furniture; over time its worn appearance will be even more in sympathy with the style of the garden.*

LEFT *Beneath the dense shade of a vine-covered arbor, all the elements that make up this tranquil scene – well-used wicker baskets, old cane chair, and straw sunhat – create the feeling that time has stood still.*
CENTER *A rich tapestry of yellow-flowering rue, purple-flowered thyme, and dark salvias cover the courtyard in front of this medieval house, just as they probably did several hundred years ago.*
BELOW *In this old greenhouse, which is no longer used for propagation, nature has taken control; nettles have rooted while moss obscures the roof panes. Traditional wooden-handled tools, which are casually propped against the shelving, provide strong visual links with the past.*

A *sense of the past*

A gnarled apple tree leaning against an old brick privy speaks of a bygone age when comforts were few but the pace of life was slower. Part of the appeal of country gardens is their link with the past. Understanding how the garden was originally used, and the essential role it played in the life of its inhabitants, gives it a value that is worth preserving. Country gardeners have never been overly concerned with trends, preferring time-honored traditions and simple style to the vicissitudes of fashion. In the past, practicality and need governed the garden; for example, in medieval cottage gardens there was no expanse of lawn (which would have been considered a complete waste of space), and the ground was almost entirely used for growing vegetables and herbs. Familiar flowers such as foxgloves, peonies, pinks, and roses, which have been grown and loved for generations, provide a sense of continuity and give the impression that, in a fast-changing world, some things are reassuringly the same.

Perfect
STRUCTURES

N O GARDEN IS MERELY an assemblage of plants. Where would a rambling rose be without its mellow stone wall acting as both support and backdrop? First come the bones of the design, that is the walls, gates, patios, paths, and buildings. These help define the character of the garden all year round, link it with the house, and provide a foil for the softer, freer forms of plants. A stone wall with small ferns in its crevices makes the boundary between garden and landscape as much an attractive link as a division, while an open post-and-rail fence allows the garden to merge with the land beyond. Country gardens often contain old buildings, such as henhouses, fallen into disuse. These might be restored for their original purpose, left as weathered features, or converted to a new use – a privy could become a wine cellar, a disused wash house an artist's studio.

LEFT *The hard landscaping in this garden has been overlaid with a casual planting of herbaceous plants, creating a relaxed atmosphere. A more formal scene could have been achieved by planting clipped topiary shapes and standard roses in a single color.*
ABOVE *Brick paths and edging add sophistication and structure to this generously planted country plot. Solid paths mean you can enjoy the sights and scents of the garden even on the wettest of days.*

The way an enclosure reveals – or masks – a dwelling can make an alluring first impression to visitors.

Few sights are more intriguing than a tucked-away house or cottage, almost hidden by a high hedge, or a tangle of tall grasses and wild flowers half-glimpsed through an ancient iron gate speckled with rust. The way an enclosure reveals – or masks – a dwelling and its garden can make an alluring first impression to the approaching visitor. A hedge, wall, or fence is so much more than a mere boundary marker. It frames the composition of the house and garden, and creates a textured yet regular background to offset planting. On the practical side, some types of enclosure offer shelter and screening for both people and plants, a support for climbing and scrambling plants, or a division to keep livestock in – or out.

Historically, people all over the world have used local materials and construction techniques to make boundary divisions, for reasons of economy and convenience – brick in clay areas, wood in forested regions, dry stone walls assembled from irregular stones found on steep hillsides where it would be impossible to carry up cement or quarried stones. If you are lucky enough to have a garden surrounded by a mature hedge or lichen-encrusted wall, retain it; its age will lend dignity to the plot. For repairs to an existing wall or fence, seek the same type of materials as originally used: local stone, the same kind of wood (unless it is to be painted), old salvaged bricks if you can find them.

A new structure will look more established and appropriate if it harmonizes with both the surrounding countryside and the house. Choosing local materials and vernacular styles, or hedging plants typical of the region, helps the boundary to fit its context and look like part of the landscape. If a hard surface seems too pristine and raw, you can speed up the aging process by painting it with a diluted solution of live yogurt and water or potting mix and water, which will encourage the spread of lichens.

A mellow brick wall provides an ideal background and support for the shell-pink blooms of the climbing rose 'New Dawn,' which flowers repeatedly from midsummer to fall. The heavy wooden door is left permanently open to reveal the rugosa rose with its large, sugar-pink blooms and to welcome new visitors, as it has for generations, to a secret garden beyond.

Walls, fences, and hedges

Stone or brick walls around a garden add a sense of solidity and, if they are high, of privacy and security. To the gardener, they not only protect the garden from intrusive animals but offer the opportunity to grow a huge variety of climbers and wall shrubs. These benefit from the wall's support, shelter, and retained warmth, and thicken over time to cloak the wall and soften the garden's boundary. Low walls can be capped or topped in a variety of decorative ways: half hoops of iron set into the top level of stones or bricks are ornamental without looking too fussy; they visually heighten the wall while at the same time allowing a view of the garden within. If the house has decorative brickwork, this could be echoed in the garden walls – for example, by placing diagonally halved bricks, pointed side up, on the top level. Copestones give a more formal, well-rounded appearance to a wall and extend its life by minimizing water infiltration from above.

In areas where flints are naturally abundant, they are a cheap but highly durable building material; they may be used whole or with one side flaked off to reveal the black core beneath. They make sturdy walls in subdued tones of gray that complement nearby rough paths and hedges. The subtle shades and fascinating textures of flint walls make them a good background to offset strong shapes such as topiary cones or towering angelica or the rich colors of oriental poppies (*Papaver orientale*), red-berried pyracantha, or purple-leaved smokebush (*Cotinus coggygria* 'Royal Purple').

LEFT *A wooded hillside has been coaxed into becoming a garden through the use of terracing, in which each level is edged with local stone. This type of stone walling has been used for centuries as its durability and character have a lasting value unaffected by fashion.*
BELOW *The beauty of simple stone has been lovingly used in creating this herringbone-patterned wall that is both practical and rich in texture. Pennywort finds a toe-hold among the crevices, its round, smooth leaves contrasting with the rough stone.*

Fences are less durable and impregnable than solid walls, but they offer endless creative possibilities. There are many different types and styles, or you could have one made to your own design; wooden fences may be left their natural color, stained to enhance the grain, or painted – perhaps to match the house or outdoor furniture; they can be used alone or in conjunction with a hedge. Some types of fencing, such as post-and-rail, allow virtually uninterrupted views into and out of the garden, while others offer discreet slits or narrow gaps to afford tantalizing glimpses of what lies beyond.

Rustic poles made from rough, unsawn lumber (sometimes with the bark left on) look simple and unpretentious, but have a relatively short life span. They can be assembled in a crisscross pattern, anchored diagonally between horizontal poles at top and bottom, or set more simply straight across in three rows between uprights. All wooden fencing should be treated with preservative.

In medieval Europe, wattle fences – often known as hurdles – were popular since they could be constructed from local wood such as hazel and were easily erected. Made from interwoven and split

FAR LEFT *Artless and unassuming,
woven wattle fencing is well suited to a
country garden where it brings a
timeless, traditional quality. An added
advantage is that it can be erected
quickly for an instant boundary and
strong textural interest.*
LEFT *An open fence of rustic poles gives
height and structure to an informal hedge
of guelder roses (*Viburnum opulus*).*
BELOW *Low post-and-rail fencing
acts as a simple reminder not to stray
too close to the water, while giving an
uninterrupted view of the plants and
countryside beyond.*

stems, wattle is excellent as a windbreak to protect plants because it is semipermeable and so filters the force of the wind; solid barriers, by contrast, deflect the air and so create pockets of turbulence. With its rustic, irregular appearance and woven texture, wattle adds a country flavor to a garden immediately. It does not have a long life span, but is ideal used alongside a newly planted hedge: by the time the hedge has grown up and thickened out, the wattle will have started to deteriorate.

In North America and Europe, low picket fencing has been popular for many centuries. It frames a garden's abundant planting without dominating or obstructing the views in or out. Plants push through the gaps and spill over the top in a casual, generous manner,

BELOW *A striking and harmonious image is created by this picket fence and collection of different-colored lilacs. The gaps in the fence allow the lilacs to grow freely and spill onto the path.*

softening its crisp, vertical lines. Picket fences are typically painted white, but are sometimes the same color as the exterior paintwork of the house, which helps to link the house with the garden to form a cohesive, harmonious design.

Hedges make excellent living boundaries and divisions in a country garden, providing good protection and shelter from wind, a textured background for other plants, and a year-round structural skeleton. Mixed-species hedges provide a changing tapestry of effects through the seasons and are perfect if you want to encourage wildlife because they offer a diversity of nesting sites and food sources. Such a hedge might include oak, holly, hawthorn, and wild rose, perhaps with ivy and wild clematis scrambling through it. You

Picket fences frame a garden's abundant planting without dominating or obstructing the views in or out.

ABOVE *In this hedge, some of the growth has been bent into a circle, creating an ingenious window in a living wall. A bower has been erected close to the hedge to create the feeling of an outside room.*
RIGHT *The scene beyond the end of this path is emphasized by the straight, clipped lines of the hedge, which contrasts with the tall trees and romping roses.*

can introduce variations in height by allowing some of the hedging plants to grow unchecked as trees. In country gardens, people sometimes grow productive trees such as apples and hazels in their hedges to make use of all the land they possess.

A clipped, single-species hedge, such as yew, holly, hornbeam, or copper beech, has a uniform appearance which is suitable for a fairly formal garden or to form a foil for free and exuberant planting. Evergreen hedges add color and texture to the garden throughout the year, while deciduous species, such as beech and oak, retain their juvenile foliage during the winter months. Provided they are clipped each year, the handsome, dried autumn leaves will cling on right through until spring, rustling in the wind.

In Italy, France, and Holland, hedges of yew or box were traditionally clipped and trained into neat geometric shapes such as cones, pyramids, and spheres, while in England humorous touches were sometimes added by shaping parts of the hedge top into peacocks, animals, and even teapots and chess pieces (see also Topiary, page 58). Where seclusion is unimportant, low hedges of lavender, box, wall germander, or cotton lavender look attractive as an edging to a path or patio or to frame beds packed with herbs, vegetables, or brightly colored annuals.

FOLLOWING PAGE *Muted green picket fencing holds back encroaching shrubs and acts as a sympathetic background to the thickly planted cosmos that flowers happily all summer under neatly trained standard fruit trees.*

BELOW *This slow-growing beech hedge has been trained into a substantial arch, which frames the countryside beyond and forms a striking foil for a spectacular* Magnolia stellata.

Garden gates

A gate is one of the first objects to come into view when you approach a garden, and it instantly makes a statement about both its owner and the garden that lies beyond it. An open trellis gate painted sky blue and yellow might suggest an artistic, extrovert gardener and offers an alluring foretaste of the garden. A tall, solid gate might be the choice of a more private person who wants to keep a secret haven hidden from the public gaze. The medieval countryman probably gave little thought to his gate; as long as it kept domestic animals in and other animals out, it did its job. Today, by contrast – with such a wide range of materials and designs – there are many decisions to make.

The guiding principle for choosing a gate is that it should blend in harmoniously with its adjoining wall, fence, or hedge. In a fence, a wooden gate of the same style and wood continues the theme, while a simple, robust design works well in a mixed hedge. Gates can be painted to match the woodwork of the house, making a visual echo; there are solid gates for complete seclusion or open designs to allow views in and out. In a brick or stone wall, a metal gate in a plain or ornate pattern complements the wall's solidity and authority. This could be painted black, an unobtrusive color such as gray or dark green, or treated to look as if it is ancient and mottled with verdigris.

If you want to make a gate more distinctive or prominent, one way is to frame it within an arch. Depending on the style of the garden, this might be of formal wrought iron, sturdy stone or brick, painted wooden fretwork, or rough rustic poles. Train scented climbers, such as honeysuckle, roses, or summer jasmine, over the arch so that you can enjoy their fragrance each time you pass through. You can train shoots from an adjacent hedge up and over a gate, making a green archway. Evergreens such as holly and yew are ideal for this because they create a solid structure all year round.

A front gate that is in regular use should be well maintained, but gates that are used infrequently or not at all may be left to acquire a dilapidated charm. A wooden gate with peeling paintwork, perhaps even hanging by one hinge, has an artless look. A metal gate held fast by scrambling and twining plants – so that it has no hope of being opened – suggests a secret garden and lush abundance, adding a tone of carefree, haphazard splendor.

If you want a gate that is a little out of the ordinary, it is worth visiting salvage yards or auctions as well as retailers of garden architecture. It may also be fairly inexpensive, and certainly more satisfying, to have a gate made to your own design. A blacksmith can construct a simple iron gate, and many carpenters will enjoy the opportunity of making an original wooden gate.

Patios and decks

Whether you work hard at tending your garden, prefer to potter at a leisurely pace among the plants, or simply sit and relax, you will be using the hard surfaces underfoot all the time. Patios, paths, and steps play a key role, fulfilling both practical and design functions, joining different areas of the garden and providing a visual link to unify the overall design.

In urban gardens, the entire area is often paved, so patios are typically associated with town plots, but they have their place in country gardens, too. A paved terrace next to the house provides the perfect spot for alfresco dining and entertaining, while a patio tucked away in a secluded corner offers a quiet retreat in which to read or daydream undisturbed. A patio or terrace often forms a transitional space between house and garden, linking the hard, architectural lines and materials of the house with the more fluid shapes and softer textures of plants.

If you are creating a new patio, consider mixing materials, such as brick and flint, to make an area that blends in gently with its surroundings, and eases the transition from house to garden. Remember, a patio does not have to be of a distinct geometric shape – a rigid rectangle may sit oddly amid the sprawling plants and wild charm of a country setting. Experiment by marking out different shapes with string and pegs; make the edge staggered, irregular, or gently curved, perhaps combining stone with cobbles or pebbles, or brick with gravel to create a soft shift of textures and an outline that merges into plants or long grass beyond.

You can soften the look of an existing patio by removing one or two paving slabs at random intervals and improving the soil below so that you can plant directly into the gaps. Choose herbs and other scented plants to spill over the edges of the paving and site them so that you can enjoy their fragrance as you sit. Include plants that have leaves with interesting textures, too – downy lady's mantle (*Alchemilla mollis*), filigree love-in-a-mist (*Nigella damascena*), felty lamb's ears (*Stachys byzantina*). On a patio, you can appreciate them close by and feel the foliage between your fingers.

Where the ground is uneven or boggy, a raised wooden deck makes an attractive and practical alternative to a traditional stone or brick terrace. Decks are particularly suitable for warm, dry areas, although they can be used in other climates, provided that they are constructed from pressure-treated hardwood. Decks may be left the natural color of the wood or stained to complement the house; the boards can also be laid in simple geometric patterns to provide additional texture and interest.

A patio tucked away in a secluded corner offers a quiet retreat in which to read or daydream undisturbed.

LEFT *The wooden pergola, covered in the sweetly scented rose 'Albertine,' offers protection from the elements, transforming the brick terrace into an additional outdoor room.*
ABOVE *A solid wooden deck built at second-floor level gives a bird's-eye view of the garden and countryside beyond. At this height the air is cooler, making the deck a refuge from the intense heat.*

A path can be laid to draw attention to fine views, a handsome tree, a tranquil pool, a solitary seat.

Paths and steps

What could be more inviting than a mellow, worn path leading you into the garden, its edges softened by mats of creeping thyme, sprawling purple sage, or bushy lavender, buzzing with bees? The course of a path suggests the direction a visitor might take around the garden, so it can be laid to draw attention to particular features – fine views, a handsome tree, a tranquil pool, a solitary seat. Wide paths offer a place in which to stroll and converse, while narrow, meandering paths beg for solo exploration.

When deciding on materials for a path, remember that the first priority is for it to be stable and comfortable underfoot. A path that will frequently bear a loaded wheelbarrow needs to be durable with a strong foundation. In traditional country gardens, paths were often no more than simple beaten earth, but these tend to become slippery in wet weather. Sometimes, cinders from the fire were

scattered and trodden down as a cheap path, but this also tends to be too insubstantial to make a satisfactory, hardwearing surface.

In a country garden, uniform modern materials such as concrete paving stones or engineering bricks can look out of place. A softer approach may be called for, perhaps using old bricks, local stone slabs, rounded cobblestones, or a loose material such as pea gravel or forest bark. As with other structures, materials should harmonize with the house and the overall style of the garden – for example, in a woodland setting, forest bark or wood chips make an attractive and appropriate path that complements informal plantings and looks good under trees. If the path runs between beds, it is best edged with wooden shuttering or sawn logs to keep the chips in place.

Bricks are very versatile for paths (and patios), their size and shape making it possible for them to be laid in different patterns, such as herringbone or basketweave; try to discover if there are particular patterns traditionally used in your area. In areas with very severe

LEFT *Sea pebbles add an extra textural dimension to this paved area. Used in two different ways, they create year-round interest while enhancing the blues and grays of the planting.*
CENTER *Paths twisting through the borders make a small garden appear larger than it actually is. Wooden shutters prevent soil from spilling onto the gravel path.*
ABOVE *Simple grass paths, flanked by profusely flowering hydrangeas, open onto an unfussy sweep of lawn, creating a verdant woodland atmosphere.*

ABOVE *Irregular flagstones act as a transition from lawn to a hard, smooth path and protect the grass from wear and tear. The uneven look of the stones complements the rustic gate and the haphazard flower planting within.*
RIGHT *Bricks laid straight into the earth with no edging divide this vegetable patch into neat sections, allowing easy access to the produce while retaining an informal look.*

winters, bricks may be damaged by frost, but more durable pavers are also available. For a more formal look, local stone paving is very attractive and weathers well with age. It is usually expensive, but there are also reconstituted stone paving tiles of good quality. In some regions, granite paving blocks may be available; these form a less even surface than stone slabs but are extremely hard-wearing and their rough texture sits well in a country garden.

In coastal gardens, gravel paths fit the mood and allow plants to grow up through them, softening the boundary between path or seating area and border. As with other loose materials, gravel should be retained by wooden shuttering or edging blocks to prevent it from spilling over onto beds and borders. Gravel is available in a variety of colors from white and gray through to buff, browns, and black to suit different styles and settings. It is noisy underfoot, which can be an advantage if you like to be alerted to the approach of a visitor.

FAR LEFT *Worn natural stone steps glow in the evening sunshine and add a touch of formality to the garden. By separating the flights of steps with lawn, a striking contrast of color and texture is created.*
LEFT *A gently sloping path has been made safe in all weathers by interspersing old railroad ties with gravel. The different textures of the wood and stone offset the lavender, as well as being attractive in their own right.*
BELOW *Soft mounds of sun-bleached pennisetum growing on each side of a short flight of steps soften their hard edges, making them appear less formal. The small bricks are strengthened by being edged with tiles.*

Having changes of level in a garden can make it feel more intriguing and livelier. As you climb a flight of steps, a new vista is revealed or an unexpected corner comes into view. The design and materials of steps contribute to the overall atmosphere: a narrow flight that twists its way out of sight up a slope suggests a secret destination, perhaps a woodland glade; broad steps seem open and inviting, a more distinct transition to another area of the garden. Hard materials such as stone slabs or pavers are most durable; use old, worn stone if you can find it, for its uneven surface will add a mellow, weathered look to the garden. In a woodland garden, wooden steps, made from heavy railroad ties or seasoned logs backfilled with soil, look more appropriate.

Steps provide plenty of cracks and crevices for small plants, helping to integrate the hard texture of the steps with the surrounding land. Choose low-growing plants such as small ferns, saxifrages, and sempervivums, as well as creeping thymes and hummocks of white and pink Mexican daisies (*Erigeron karvinskianus*), that will not impede people's passage.

Garden buildings

Many country gardens contain an old building that is a reminder of some past function or fashion – a crumbling brick henhouse, an old dairy or wash house, a weathered wooden tool shed, a humble outhouse, or something rather more ornamental such as a summerhouse or gazebo. For some people, it may be tempting to tear down such a structure, particularly if it looks very neglected and dilapidated, but these buildings add character and a sense of history to a garden as well as being of practical use.

Up until the early part of the twentieth century, many people in rural areas kept a pig or cow on their small patch of land, so some gardens still retain a small piggery or cowshed. Left to the effects of time and nature, these can become very attractive buildings, with moss-covered roof tiles and ivy-clad walls that soften their utilitarian nature. Although they may be unsuitable for conversion to human use – piggeries are typically squat, with low entranceways, for example – they can make good storehouses for tools or firewood, or even as safe night shelters for keeping ducks and chickens (see also Livestock, pages 98–101).

With an unadorned, battered exterior and gloomy interior still harboring neat stacks of old clay pots and smelling of potting mix, an ancient tool shed has a timeless quality and simplicity. Sheds have many functions: they may be used to store garden equipment, with rows of hooks supporting old but much-loved tools, as a potting shed with a sturdy workbench, or as dry storage for logs or coal; as long as there is a window, a shed may even be suitable as a small study or workroom. Provided it has good proportions and is basically of sound construction, even quite a neglected shed may be worth restoring. Any restoration work should be in keeping with the original design and materials to retain the character of the building.

Coalhouses and wood piles were often solidly built and quite large, roomy enough to hold a supply of firewood for the duration of the winter. For houses that still have an open fireplace or a wood-burning stove, a dry storage place is to be prized, so a building like this may well be kept for its original purpose. Firewood stores tend not to have windows, so they are less suitable for conversion, although windows could be added, provided that they complement the style of building.

Before the advent of indoor plumbing, old houses usually had an outdoor privy in the garden. In poor households, these were typically constructed of wood, while more affluent houses might have had larger privies built of stone, with a dividing brick wall. Privies often lend themselves to conversion into storage areas.

Moss-covered roof tiles and ivy-clad walls soften the utilitarian nature of old cowsheds and outhouses.

LEFT *An unassuming wooden shed with shutters has aged to become an intregal part of this garden, which burgeons with clouds of hydrangeas, feathery astilbes, hostas, roses, and daisies.*
ABOVE *Ivy, pittosporum, and the grass gardener's garters have enveloped and claimed this hut, so that it seems almost to have grown up with the plants.*

Alternatively, by adding a stable door so the top half can be left open to let in light and air, an outhouse can be turned into a child's playhouse, if it is large enough.

Functional buildings can be made more attractive as garden features, and integrated into the overall scheme, if plants are grown around or over them. Tall, wild plants such as bright sunflowers and felty mullein look particularly good in such a setting, while climbers such as ivy, rambling roses, clematis, and morning glories can be trained to scramble over the structure so that it looks as if it has itself grown out of the land along with the plants. Some types of structure look their best with natural or stained woodwork (treated with preservative), while others call out for stylish paintwork – perhaps in muted blue-gray or dark green to blend in with the garden, or in pristine white, with the windows and door picked out in a fresh green, soft blue, or defining black.

LEFT *Handmade clay pots are far more attractive than mass-produced plastic ones. These have all have been scrubbed and washed, ready to be used again for cuttings in the coming months.*

ABOVE *This simple wooden hut is a dry and convenient place for storing garden tools. The lean-to gives shade in summer and cover for logs in winter.*

BELOW *This rustic round house provides shelter from the elements beneath its snug thatched roof. The wattle hurdles and rough poles are in harmony with its forest surroundings.*

CENTER *A privy has been carefully converted into a summerhouse. Submerged among silver birch, hollyhocks, foxgloves, catnip, and campanula, it offers a quiet retreat in which to read and contemplate.*

RIGHT *A treehouse is exciting whether seen from the ground half-hidden by branches, or as you perch inside it like a bird and survey your domain. Ivy has been allowed to smother this treehouse, almost bringing it to life.*

Although many country gardens were primarily practical in the past, they were not without their more decorative buildings. Whimsical follies and elaborate gazebos were largely confined to relatively grand estates, but simpler structures such as summerhouses have enjoyed periods of great popularity. In the seventeenth century, idealized notions of pastoral and rural life held sway among the wealthier members of European society, resulting in a vogue for "rustic" buildings made of undressed wood.

The late nineteenth century saw a return to this fashion – a summerhouse was considered an essential feature in every middle-class garden in Victorian England. All kinds of fantastical and exotic styles were created and constructed, varying from the oriental tearoom to the alpine chalet. Some were so ambitious that they were even built on a kind of turntable that allowed the house to be

rotated so the occupants could enjoy different views and be turned toward the sun. The most popular were those built of rustic materials – rough, unsawn branches and slim logs, usually with their bark intact. The roof might be thatched or made of bracken or heather, and the "windows" were generally unglazed and simply open to the elements.

Nowadays, few people would go to such lengths, and very elaborate constructions might seem at odds with the carefree simplicity of a country garden. A simple clapboard summerhouse is more in keeping, with windows on two sides to allow views of the garden, and a sturdy slate or tile roof to stave off the elements. In a wild garden or orchard, a building made of rustic poles will harmonize with the long grass dotted with wildflowers and bulbs and the rough textures of old, gnarled fruit trees.

A simple clapboard summerhouse, with a sturdy slate or tile roof, is in keeping with the carefree simplicity of the country garden.

Perfect PLANTING

*T*HE IMAGE OF A COUNTRY GARDEN is conjured up immediately at the mention of certain plants: foxgloves, poppies, peonies, sweet peas, roses, and honeysuckle – the list of names is a soothing mantra for the stressed city dweller. Many of these plants have a quiet charm and easy grace rather than being showy specimens trying to hog the limelight; they are as familiar, reliable, and comforting as old friends. Think of rock roses spilling onto a stone path, silvery lavender shimmering with scent and hovering bees, walls thickly cloaked with glossy ivy or pale pink clematis. Often, they may be indigenous plants that also grow naturally outside the garden walls, helping to give the garden a sense of belonging to the landscape. Plants are the life and the heart of a garden, setting the tone and atmosphere and offering us endless pleasures and surprises.

LEFT *Roses interspersed with billowing clumps of* Campanula lactiflora *and spikes of purple toadflax* (Linaria purpurea) *epitomize the country garden where plants are allowed to place themselves at will and find their own ideal companions.*

ABOVE *With its subtly varying flower color, the sweetly scented rose 'Felicia' complements the majestic common foxglove. In the shadows of a wood, colors appear deeper and more powerful.*

BELOW *The lushness of this planting conveys a feeling of well-being and abundance. Catnip (Nepeta) and geraniums thread their way through each other, while white iris and yellow yarrow (Achillea) add a lively touch.*
CENTER *Deep flowerbeds allow plants to grow into generous clumps to make a positive statement. The blue globe thistle (Echinops) and yarrow heads can be left uncut to provide winter interest.*
RIGHT *An arch covered with roses and honeysuckle and box topiary cones are medieval elements that survive in cottage gardens today, adding scent and structure to a vegetable and flower garden.*

Creating country style

The charm of a country garden lies in its informality, a feeling of lush abundance, fluidity, and artless splendor. Traditionally, modest country gardens had no lawns because every inch of space was needed for growing valuable herbs, vegetables, and flowers. Borders were deep, and as the country gardener was less interested in design than in productivity, vegetables were grown in easily accessible rows, while flowers and herbs were massed together in an apparently chaotic way and allowed to seed themselves around. For many people, this dense tapestry effect is the epitome of country border style, and even the most accomplished gardeners recognize that the happy accident can be as successful as the

carefully planned scheme. There is often great art in creating such an informal, natural, and spontaneous look, however, and thoughtful planning, a cohesive sense of style, and well-directed maintenance are essential if an enchanting display is not to tumble over into a shapeless disorder.

Draw inspiration from the natural features and characteristics of your site and of the area. Notice the plants that occur locally and how they grow together in natural associations. A nearby area of woodland might suggest ideas for a small grove of deciduous trees, underplanted with ferns, bluebells, and wood anemones. A local wet meadow or natural pool could provide associations of bog and marginal plants or moisture-loving trees for a waterlogged patch of the garden or the edge of a pond.

Even accomplished gardeners recognize that the happy accident can be as successful as the carefully planned scheme.

Choose plants that thrive in the given conditions, rather than battling with nature, to create a garden that looks harmonious and natural.

Understanding nature

The foundation of growing plants successfully lies in understanding the climate, soil, and growing conditions of your area in general and your garden in particular. Country gardens are typically more prone to climatic extremes than town gardens, which are usually more sheltered and protected from severe frosts or winds because of the concentration of buildings. In open country, gardens may be exposed to strong winds that dry and scorch plants, especially in coastal regions, and temperatures may fluctuate wildly. Frost can be especially damaging to tender young shoots and new growth. Soil may vary enormously within the garden – for example, ranging from free-draining chalk to heavy clay. Before selecting plants, it is best to make a thorough assessment of the conditions on your site, including soil type and pH, aspect, minimum and maximum temperatures, and the location of frost pockets.

Most gardeners inherit a garden with some long-established plants, which are good indicators of the growing conditions. For example, aromatic plants usually like free-draining, dry, sunny conditions where their roots will not get wet, while hostas, astilbes, pulmonarias, and phlox grow happily in cooler, shadier, damp spots. In addition to providing planting ideas, wildflowers in surrounding fields and woods signal that cultivated plants of the same family could do well in the garden. Choosing plants that thrive in the given conditions – rather than battling with nature by trying to change those conditions drastically – keeps maintenance to a minimum and helps create a garden that looks harmonious and natural.

LEFT *Golden helianthus, flowering abundantly in the North American countryside, demonstrates the effectiveness and impact of block planting. The related common sunflower (*Helianthus annuus*) and the Jerusalem artichoke (*H. tuberosus*) were both valued by Native Americans as a source of food.*

ABOVE *Delicate poppies have self-seeded in the dry, open patches between the trees of this grove. They look their best in such exposed, sunlit positions where their reds and pinks appear more intense against the cool shadows cast by the trees.*

BELOW *Surrounded by hedges and large trees, the framework of this long plot has been kept simple by placing a path centrally; the plants spilling across it soften its appearance. At the far end, a glazed urn acts as a focal point.*

Establishing the framework

In an informal or semiwild garden, it is especially important to have a well-designed framework to give shape and structure to free and exuberant planting. This is partly formed by the layout and buildings, but also by long-term and architectural plants, particularly trees and shrubs. These are the bones of the garden, providing all-year interest and a satisfying composition of shapes even when most other plants have little to offer. Once established, they add weight and dignity to a garden. In addition to their ornamental qualities – blossom, foliage, form, decorative bark – trees have immense potential as design elements: they can be used to frame a view, line a driveway, provide a living shade canopy over a wooden seat, half-conceal a secret corner of the garden, or arch over water to create fascinating reflections.

The qualities of a tree or shrub affect the choice of its ideal position – the dark pyramid of a holly tree (*Ilex*) has a strong impact seen against the sky or the muted grays of a stone wall, while the ghostly bark of a silver birch (*Betula*) or the glaucous foliage of a gum tree (*Eucalyptus*) are better offset against the dark background of a yew hedge or dense woods beyond the garden boundary. Include shrubs of contrasting forms for a dynamic and balanced design, but use some plants of similar shape to make visual echoes and lead the eye from point to point around the garden. Architectural perennials can be used in the same way – the silver spires of mullein (*Verbascum*) or the towering flowerheads of globe thistle (*Echinops*) make emphatic verticals, while many grasses form dense clumps with whiplike leaves and striking plumes of flowers that catch the light as they sway in the wind.

ABOVE *A mature hedge acts as a permanent background to the various shrubs that form the skeleton of the garden. Showy peony-flowered poppies* (Papaver somniferum) *and delicate spikes of linaria stand out against their subdued background.*

ABOVE RIGHT *Mullein has long been a favorite in cottage gardens. Its strongly architectural shape adds height to a border, while its downy gray leaves look attractive growing out of gravel paths. It is long flowering and happily spreads itself in the dryest of situations.*

A garden for all seasons

ABOVE *Forget-me-nots (*Myosotis*)
and apple blossom herald the longer,
warmer days of spring. Forget-me-nots
as blue as the sky are a valuable space-
filler during late spring after daffodils
have flowered and before perennials
have grown to their full size.*

RIGHT *Many poppies such as these*
Papaver somniferum *develop attractive
seedheads after flowering, which add
interest well into winter – especially
when covered in frost – as do the thistle-
like heads of sea hollies (*Eryngium*),
which fade elegantly with age.*

Although you may spend most time in the garden in mild springs
and balmy falls, a garden that can be seen from the house should
offer plenty to delight all year round. Including plants that have a
distinctive form or evergreen foliage allows you to create a
composition that will remain pleasing from month to month.
However, beware of having too many plants such as stiff conifers
that hardly seem to alter as the year passes as this can look too static;
plants that change with the seasons are what give a garden vitality.
If the garden is small, it is especially important that every piece of
ground is well used rather than accommodating a dazzling but brief
display, then being a non-event for a large part of the year. Shrubs
and perennials can be intermingled with annuals scattered as seed,
or underplanted with bulbs – try small-leaved bulbs such as rock
narcissus and crocus around the base of violas or chrysanthemums,
so that the bulbs' cheerful flowers brighten the gray days of early
spring before their companion plant has started to romp away.

Plants that have attractive foliage usually provide a longer season
of interest than those grown for their flowering display alone. A
shady spot is the ideal home for many ferns such as the tall and

impressive royal fern (*Osmunda regalis*) or the evergreen *Asplenium scolopendrium* 'Marginatum' with long, narrow fronds that are crimped and cut at the edges. Roses may be best loved for their beautiful blooms, but look for those that have attractive leaves, too, such as *Rosa glauca* with its violet-gray foliage. Some also give pleasure well into the fall with decorative autumn hips such as *R. moyesii*, which becomes covered in brilliant scarlet fruits, or *R.* 'Fru Dagmar Hastrup' with round, tomatolike hips. Amelanchiers are shrubs or trees that give excellent value. They never grow huge, and provide a changing palette of colors through the year. In early spring, the branches look as though they have been sprinkled with snow. In midsummer, scarlet berries develop in small bunches. The leaves are a delight in the fall, as they turn a wonderful warm crimson touched with gold.

Many plants have attractive seedheads which continue to look good long after the flowers have finished, especially with a covering of frost; the lollipop heads of alliums act as vertical punctuation marks in a border of low-growing plants. Ornamental grasses often give good value for a long period – there are golden, striped, blue,

LEFT *Shrubs grown at the back of a bed help protect perennials and annuals from harsh winds and intense sunlight, allowing them to extend their flowering period. This is also helped by regular deadheading.*
ABOVE RIGHT *Tough rugosa roses make an effective hedge for a garden as they flower repeatedly and then produce magnificent clusters of large hips. The color of the roses is picked up by sweet William (*Dianthus barbatus*).*
RIGHT *Fast-growing blanket flowers (*Gaillardia × grandiflora*), one of the longest-flowering perennials, catch the evening sunlight. They also tolerate poor growing conditions, as does the* Salvia microphylla *beside them.*

or reddish-brown forms and even a black, grass-like perennial, *Ophiopogon planiscapus* 'Nigrescens.' Some have long-lasting flower spikes such as golden oats (*Stipa gigantea*), with airy, silver-gold panicles taller than a man, or fluffy hare's tail grass (*Lagurus ovatus*).

Winter may not be the most colorful time in the garden, but evergreen shrubs help to make a garden feel clothed on the shortest winter days. Buckthorn (*Rhamnus alaternus* 'Argenteovariegata') has small, variegated leaves that will cheer the barest of dry corners beside a house. The winter garden need not be without its flowers. *Prunus × subhirtella* 'Autumnalis' has sugar-pink, fluffy flowers from late fall until early spring, while some viburnums (such as *Viburnum farreri* or *V. × bodnantense*) flower in winter and are strongly scented. Grown close to the house, they act as a cheerful reminder that the garden is never entirely dormant.

Evergreen shrubs help to make a garden feel clothed even on the shortest winter days.

LEFT *In a wild garden, old man's beard* (Clematis vitalba) *can be allowed to romp over bushes. On dark winter days the fluffy seedheads bring an enchanting lightness to the garden and provide a valuable food source for birds.*

LEFT *Hoar frost turns any garden into a magical place, covering each stem and leaf with a coat of ice that sparkles and catches the weak winter sunshine. To achieve such a scene, cut perennials down in spring rather than in late fall.*
BELOW *The first and last frosts of the year dramatically paint outlines on the deciduous leaves of* Passiflora caerulea *and* Clematis *'Ascotiensis.'*

You could also consider growing trees and shrubs that have colorful or patterned stems and bark, to introduce a flash of strong color when there are few flowers to compete. Several Tibetan cherry trees (*Prunus serrula*) grown together, with their garnet-colored, silky bark, will enliven a wild patch in any garden. A small thicket of red-stemmed dogwoods (*Cornus alba* 'Sibirica') or the arresting lime-green form (*C. stolonifera* 'Flaviramea') makes a striking winter feature, especially when seen in contrast against a dark wall. If you have the space, you might want to include silver birches, such as *Betula utilis* var. *jacquemontii* with its dazzling white bark, snake-bark maples (*Acer pennsylvanicum*), or gum trees (*Eucalyptus*), some of which have extraordinary patterned, peeling, or textured bark.

ABOVE *The formality of topiary and the strong lines of clipped box hedges have been softened by the juxtaposition of plants with a loose or relaxed habit, such as columbines (*Aquilegia*), love-in-a-mist (*Nigella damascena*), and delphiniums grown in a random manner.*
RIGHT *Generous billows of box clipped into gentle mounds surround deciduous trees and form such a striking picture that you hardly notice that it is winter. Taller, crisply shaped cones lift the eye and contrast well with the warm tones of the beech hedge.*

The art of topiary

As far back as the first century, the Romans decorated their gardens with intricate topiary shapes made from clipped and trained plants. Animals, people, even ships were made out of cypress (*Cupressus sempervirens*). Topiary provides living sculpture in the garden; usually formed from evergreens such as yew (*Taxus baccata*) or box (*Buxus sempervirens*), it looks attractive all year round – even blanketed in snow – and combines formality with humor, so it is no wonder that it never really goes out of fashion. It enjoyed a revival in Renaissance Italy in the fifteenth century and, from Florence, its popularity spread across Europe, with each nation adapting styles to suit their particular tastes; migrants from Europe spread the art to North America. In the seventeenth century, yew became increasingly popular in northern Europe as it withstood the hard winters better than cypress or some of the more tender shrubs.

Although topiary was originally a feature of grand gardens, when it fell out of favor and was deemed old-fashioned in the early nineteenth century, it lived on in simple cottage gardens where people were less concerned with what was in vogue. Now, clipped shapes such as spheres and peacocks look as much at home in a small garden nestling alongside an artisan's cottage as they do on a grand country estate. Borders thick with delphiniums, hollyhocks, poppies, and roses form an exciting contrast with the dark density of yew and the crisp precision of neatly clipped shapes.

Whether it is an elaborate figure such as an animal or a simple shape such as a cone or spiral, a piece of topiary draws the eye immediately and acts as an exclamation mark in the garden. A simple planting of, say, clove pinks or plain red tulips is made more unusual and eye-catching if they surround a single-stemmed tree clipped into a neat ball. The contrasts of height and form, color and texture serve to offset the qualities of each plant. You can draw attention to a breathtaking view beyond the garden or a particular focal point by framing it with a window cut into a boundary hedge. This is a good device for focusing the eye on a vista that, if seen in its entirety, would lose its impact. A topiary hedge, with shapes cut into the top, can also be used to obliterate an unsightly view.

In addition to providing an opportunity for the gardener to demonstrate creativity and skill in a way that can be enjoyed all year round, topiary gives a garden a sense of timelessness and continuity. Once trained and established, the living shapes often become fixtures in a garden, and long after the original creator has left, successive gardeners take up the responsibility of maintaining and nurturing a focal point that may be enjoyed by passersby as well.

Climbers and wall shrubs

Climbing plants and wall shrubs are essential features of the country garden. From Dutchman's pipe (*Aristolochia durior*) growing on a New England clapboard cottage to an ancient wisteria scrambling over the balcony of a Swiss alpine chalet, climbers soften the hard angles of buildings and structures, and anchor them to the garden and the surrounding landscape. Some also have a functional value: training shrubs and fruit trees against a wall makes good use of space, while the plants benefit from the shelter and retained warmth of the wall. In Mediterranean countries, vine-covered pergolas have long been used to offer respite from the baking sun; a simple leafy bower over a seat provides a cool, secluded spot where you can enjoy the scent of honeysuckle; an ornamental arbor, dripping with roses, becomes filled with their perfume, making it the perfect place to daydream.

Climbers grow in different ways, and this affects the type of support that they need. Some, such as sweet peas, hang onto their host by sending out tendrils. Others twine and twist, such as clematis and jasmine; these are difficult to disentangle so they may be unsuitable on supports that need periodic painting or treating with preservative. Plants such as ivies and climbing hydrangea have aerial roots or little suckers that cling onto their support; this makes them easy to grow since they can be left to wander at will over a wall or tree without having to be tied in.

Some climbers, such as wisteria and certain roses, can become very heavy in time and so need a sturdy support. Choose climbers appropriate for the situation. Most climbing roses need to be pruned and tied in to their support, so they might be suitable for growing over a trellis around a porch, whereas ramblers need little attention and will happily romp up and through mature trees. Check the average height and spread of plants when mature, too. For example, *Rosa fillipes* 'Kiftsgate' gives a magical feel as its pale, moonlike flowers hang down in clusters among the dark foliage of a tree, but it grows very large, so it is best used only where there is plenty of space.

As when planning beds and borders, apply similar principles to planting on walls and other vertical structures. Think about color, texture, foliage, seasonal interest. Grow a spring-flowering clematis alongside a rose that will bloom through summer, perhaps with a purple-leaved vine (*Vitis vinifera* 'Purpurea') to give color well into the fall. Brighten up a gloomy wall with a golden-variegated ivy (try *Hedera helix* 'Goldheart' or *H. colchica* 'Sulphur Heart'), which is shade-tolerant and offers year-round cover. Use fast-growing annuals such as morning glory (*Convolvulus tricolor* 'Heavenly Blue') to give interest while a more slow-growing climber becomes established.

ABOVE *The delicate flowers of a trained pyracantha lighten the subdued wall of a cottage, welcoming in the spring and raising the spirits. During the gloomy months of winter, clusters of brilliantly colored berries will bring color and provide food for birds.*

RIGHT *Left to its own devices, a Virginia creeper (*Parthenocissus*) has thickly coated this French barn; in time, even the roof and doors will become covered. Although it gives a wonderful rich color in the fall, its suckering, creeping habit may damage walls and roofs.*

Tapestries of color and texture

The multicolored tapestry effect of a country garden border can be dazzling, with harmonious plant associations as well as those that clash brazenly, all mingling in a riot of color. Some gardeners, however, prefer to use a more limited color scheme in their borders, with a single color or restricted color range that includes many different plants. The effect is not as casual and spontaneous, but it allows the creation of a more distinct atmosphere and impact within different parts of the garden. Cool, soft colors such as blues, mauves, and grays give a feeling of peace and tranquility, while hot colors like fiery reds and oranges suggest passion, excitement, and cheerfulness. A border planted with pale tones – perhaps pure white, soft cream, hints of peach, and muted silver-gray – appears calm and reflective but also uplifting. When planting a border in a strictly limited color range, include plants of different shapes, heights, and textures to give additional interest and variety.

Texture is an element that is frequently overlooked, but the enormous diversity of textural effects from the foliage of different plants can give great pleasure, to the touch as well as to the eye. Combine plants of contrasting textures to draw attention to their

surfaces – matte next to shiny, feathery near solid, felty near glossy. It is hard to pass by plants such as downy mullein (*Verbascum olympicum*) or fennel (*Foeniculum vulgare*) with its soft, filigree foliage without reaching out to touch them. Leaf size and form affect textural appearance, too: plant hellebores, such as *Helleborus × sternii*, with bugle (*Ajuga*) and snowdrops, the straplike leaves of the latter complementing the large, cut leaves of the hellebores. Use the regular, dense, matte background of a yew (*Taxus baccata*) hedge as a foil for the shiny, jagged, and variegated leaves of *Osmanthus heterophyllus* 'Aureomarginatus' or the airy habit of a cut-leaved elder (*Sambucus racemosa* 'Plumosa Aurea').

ABOVE *In the cool shadows of a large tree, an impressionistic picture has been painted by interweaving a small pink-flowered geranium with feverfew and using the creamy, feathery heads of astilbe to emphasize the ribbed texture of the blue hosta leaves.*

LEFT *A dry, rocky slope is the ideal place to grow vibrantly colored plants such as yellow* Asphodeline lutea, *globe-headed alliums, white and pink valerian, and dianthus, which clash beautifully.*
ABOVE *Color and texture are used to great advantage here: gray senecio contrasts with a wispy ornamental grass and the large blue-gray leaves of a cardoon (*Cynara cardunculus*). Yellow phlomis adds vibrancy and balance.*
FOLLOWING PAGE *Colorful lupine spikes stand majestically above mounds of thyme and a small-leaved geranium, whose magenta flowers are picked up by the bleeding heart (*Dicentra spectabilis*). The delphiniums are yet to flower.*

RIGHT *A garden should be remembered for its scents as well as its colors. The sultry smell of ghostly lilies hangs heavily on the still air as the evening sun sets. Lilies have been grown for their invaluable and unforgettable perfume since Egyptian times.*

ABOVE RIGHT *Honeysuckle has always been a firm favorite in country gardens. Grown close to an open window, its honey-sweet scent will fill the room. A simple arbor becomes a magical place when it is covered with fragrant honeysuckle and roses.*

FAR RIGHT *An old-fashioned Damask rose 'La Ville de Bruxelles,' whose highly scented petals are ideal for making potpourri, complements the airy flower heads of ground elder. A pernicious weed, ground elder is unwelcome in most gardens and should not be allowed to flower. The owner of this garden, however, has given up the battle of trying to eradicate it.*

The sudden whiff of a plant loved in childhood can transport you back in an instant.

The scented garden

What pleasures fragrant plants can add: the heady aroma of phlox, the honey smell of buddleia, the exquisite perfume of many roses. How delicious it is to wander among night-perfumed plants with the moon illuminating spectral flowers. (Strongly scented plants often have pale-colored petals because their perfume is designed to attract night-flying insects, such as moths, to pollinate them.) Scent is so evocative – the sudden whiff of a plant loved in childhood can transport you back in an instant. The pleasure of sitting among an abundance of flowers is doubled when those blooms perfume the still air, the clovey smell of pinks blending with the heady scent of hardy lilies, or the sweet aroma of *Paeonia lactiflora* 'Sarah Bernhardt' mingling with the old-fashioned annual mignonette (*Reseda odorata*). Also consider growing a selection of herbs together to provide a scented corner of the garden (see Herbs, pages 92–7).

Site scented plants with care – in a spot that will allow you to enjoy them to the full. Plant climbers around a doorway or window so you can smell them from the house, or train them over a pergola and relish their fragrance as you sit below. Grow fragrant plants in containers on a patio or next to a path so you can sniff the blooms as you pass. Tobacco plants (*Nicotiana*) massed beneath a window will gently perfume the room within. Sadly, some newer varieties have no fragrance, so take care to choose those with a good scent, such as *N. alata*. This is also true of other plants including many roses and sweet peas; check that you have a scented type before you buy.

Seashore and city spaces

A coastal site can be a great challenge, but potential views and moderate temperatures offer generous compensation. The main problem is salt-laden winds, which burn tender leaves and dry the soil, restricting the choice of plants. You can improve conditions by creating a shelter belt; shrubs act as a good windbreak, slowing down the wind and reducing its desiccating effects. For the perimeter, use tough shrubs that tolerate salty air – such as tamarisk (*Tamarix*), sea buckthorn (*Hippophae rhamnoides*), lavender, phlomis, cotoneaster, and escallonia. Gray-foliaged plants and those with small leaves tend to be quite resilient in the face of drying winds. Low-growing shrubs are also usually more wind-resistant; include those such as cistus and potentillas that have an especially long flowering period.

Plants of the thistle family are tough and add height and structure to a plot; grow echinops and silvery-blue sea holly (*Eryngium*) with clumps of waxy-leaved sedums, *Centranthus ruber* and *Glaucium flavum*. Low-growing plants escape the winds and can give an attractive tapestry effect. *Phuopsis stylosa*, with its umbrellas of sugar-pink flowers, can be underplanted with *Allium moly* to grow up and through its carpet of leaves, while rock roses (*Helianthemum*) give a long display of flowers all through summer. Mat-forming plants introduce different textures and help prevent soil erosion. The ferny gray leaves of *Tanacetum densum* complement the wooly texture of *Ballota pseudodictamnus*. As both are pale, they make good companions to flowers of any color, so that you can alter your color scheme of annuals from year to year while retaining these key plants.

A town garden that is planted in a country style is perhaps even more delightful for being a surprise. What a joy it is to enter a door in a high town wall and discover a garden belonging to another world. Even in a large city, you can recreate a rural feel by keeping the planting informal and generous, with climbers covering the walls to enclose the garden in greenery and plenty of plants to tumble over paths, trail from a pergola or spill from tubs and troughs.

There may not be enough space for traditional borders, but you can establish a similar effect in a courtyard by massing together large containers that are densely planted. Not all shrubs need a lot of root space either – fig trees, for example, like having their roots restricted. Climbers such as summer and winter jasmine, with rambling roses, will lure birds to make their homes, bringing sounds of the country into town. Plants that have long been associated with country gardens such as pinks, ferns, hardy geraniums, and poppies mingling in apparently unchecked abundance can make even the most hardened town dweller feel that here is a breath of the countryside.

RIGHT *This hillside garden on the Mediterranean coast is filled with fruit trees and herbs that can largely take care of themselves. The verdant foliage offers cool shade in which to walk, and the leaves of the citrus trees can be crushed as you pass by, to release their pleasing aroma. Low-growing thymes hug the ground out of the wind; their small, aromatic leaves can withstand baking sun and salt-laden air.*

Mass plants together in drifts, rather than placing them singly, to increase their allure to bees, butterflies, and other pollinating insects.

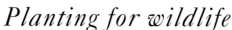

Planting for wildlife

The drowsy buzz of bees, the sound of birdsong, and the fluttering of butterflies add a feeling of vitality and harmony to sunny days spent relaxing in the garden. Without bees and other pollinating insects, some plants (such as many fruit trees, beans, and some perennials) would not set seed or yield fruit. Bees are very attracted to blue and mauve flowers, as found in lavender, catnip (*Nepeta*), campanulas, and scabious, to name but a few. Place plants together in drifts rather than individually to increase their allure.

Country people have always valued birds in the garden. In addition to being fascinating to watch and filling the air with song, birds help to control many pests – some keep aphids at bay, while others eat as many snails as they can find. Encourage birds into the garden by including a wide range of shrubs and small trees. Most birds like to make short flights from one source of cover to another. Wall shrubs and trees with dense or thorny growth such as hawthorn (*Crataegus*) or holly (*Ilex*) make ideal nesting sites for many birds, and plants with berries, for example, pyracantha, rowans (*Sorbus*), and hollies, are a vital source of food during severe weather, even attracting species which at other times might be too shy to visit a garden.

LEFT *A colorful peacock butterfly rests on a vivid yellow* Inula *flower, absorbing heat from the sun before nightfall.*
ABOVE *Large, sugar-pink oriental poppies (*Papaver orientale*), spikes of persicaria, cream iris, and Scotch thistle (*Onopordum acanthium*) with blue-gray foliage offer a wide range of nectar-filled flowers to attract bees, moths, and butterflies to this patch.*
RIGHT *Massed delphiniums stand boldly in front of a climbing rose while, at their feet, lady's mantle (*Alchemilla mollis*) and catnip (*Nepeta 'Six Hills Giant'*) sprawl over the earth. Small birds like to make their nests at the back of such densely planted borders, which offer good cover.*

Perfect PRODUCE

*F*RESHLY PICKED LETTUCE LEAVES, newly dug potatoes, and an omelet courtesy of free-range hens – what could be more satisfying and delicious than a simple meal produced by your own labors on your own patch of land? In medieval times, people in rural areas grew as much food as they could from necessity. In France, the vegetable plot traditionally took pride of place, with neat rows of beans, tomatoes, and salad crops in the front yard and flowers relegated to the rear of the house. Italian gardeners used shrubby, medicinal herbs such as hyssop and cotton lavender to edge their vegetable beds. A garden where chickens, ducks, or geese wander at will conjures up an age far removed from the horrors of intensive production methods. The country dweller's larder is not restricted to the garden, however; beyond, in hedges and woods, edible berries, nuts, and leaves as well as mushrooms can be harvested by the knowledgeable.

LEFT *Lovage, bay, fennel, and sage grow well with other kitchen herbs in a quiet and easily accessible corner of this vegetable plot. Their pungent leaves are ready for picking to add the flavor of the countryside to a simple meal.*
ABOVE *In the shelter of a stone wall, a colorful rooster stands sentinel over his domain. Domestic birds and animals help to bring a country garden to life.*

Growing vegetables

There is something immensely satisfying about well-tended rows
or blocks of healthy vegetables: a line of fat, blue-mauve cabbages,
wispy fronds of Florence fennel, earthed-up rows of potatoes, and
tall wigwams covered in scarlet-flowered beans all give a promise
of delectable meals to come. Vegetables have long been a vital part
of people's diet in rural areas, since meat was usually expensive.
The French have always been the most enthusiastic of vegetable
growers; in the sixteenth century, their delight in orderliness resulted
in plots of wonderful geometric patterns and colors – formal kitchen
gardens laid out in elaborate symmetrical designs with vegetables
enclosed by low, clipped box hedges. A simpler approach is to grow
vegetables in blocks; this makes cultivation practical and creates
bold patches of color.

LEFT *A scarecrow adds humor and an
idiosyncratic touch to a vegetable patch,
although this one looks too good natured
to frighten away many birds.*
ABOVE *Companion planting is a
tried-and-tested method of growing
vegetables with other plants to reduce
pest problems. Here, yellow marigolds
(*Tagetes*) are grown to deter pests
such as nematode worms and to attract
beneficial insects, especially hoverflies,
which feed on many pests.*

RIGHT *A well-planned vegetable garden can provide enough for a family all year round. Dwarf beans can be blanched, then frozen, and a glut of tomatoes made into sauces and relish to be enjoyed on cold winter days. Gathering the crops brings a pleasurable sense of achievement to reward all your hard work.*

*A line of fat,
blue-mauve cabbages
and earthed-up rows
of potatoes give a
promise of delectable
meals to come.*

LEFT *In the lee of a fig tree, this
Mediterranean plot includes larkspur
and sweet peas growing abundantly
among cabbages and lettuce. Where
space permits, it is worth planting
fast-growing annuals like this to
provide cut flowers for the house.*
ABOVE *Potatoes, spinach, lettuce,
cauliflower, and cabbages are packed
into a small space, with sweet peas
planted to bloom above them.*

Colorful crops

Pumpkins and squash look like extraordinary living sculptures. This pumpkin has been allowed to appropriate the garden bench, where its rich color and generous shape can be seen to full advantage.

Color need not be sacrificed for productivity in the vegetable garden – there are all sorts of colorful as well as useful crops available. The runner bean cultivar 'Painted Lady' has pretty red and white flowers, while the French bean 'Marvel of Venice' has delicate lilac flowers, later followed by glowing primrose-colored beans. Trained up an arch over a rustic seat, they make an attractive addition and are a productive way of using all the available space.

One way of dividing your plot is into blocks of colors – try growing yellow zucchini, such as 'Gold Rush,' so they ripen beside sweet-tasting 'Yellow Pear' tomatoes. Purple bush beans such as 'Royal Burgundy' are a good partner for purple kohlrabi, perhaps

LEFT *The shocking pink stems of rainbow chard are a striking feature in a flowerbed, surrounded by low-growing thymes, marjoram, or velvety* Viola tricolor *'Bowles' Black.'*
BELOW *'Alouette' endive adds color in the vegetable garden. The smooth, purple leaves, splashed with green, contrast well with feathery bronze fennel or frilly lettuces such as 'Lollo Rosso.'*

enlivened with brilliant scarlet-stemmed ruby chard, while nearby deep maroon onions (try 'Brunswick Red') ripen in the sun. The green feathery leaves of carrots are a happy companion to frilly-leaved lettuces, such as 'Red Sails,' 'Lollo Rosso,' or 'Salad Bowl.' Rainbow chard looks spectacular massed against a dark wall or hedge, its stems of shocking pink, tangerine orange, or sunshine yellow brightening even the dullest of days and producing an endless crop of edible leaves.

Some rural areas are plagued with rabbits and deer, making it necessary to fence in the vegetable patch. Chicken wire bedded into the soil and supported by posts offers a structure over which to grow plants, such as nasturtiums, zucchini, and pumpkins, to introduce color late in the season.

Planting partners and paths

Companion planting is an aspect of country folklore that makes sound practical sense in the vegetable garden. For generations, gardeners have observed that certain combinations of vegetables appear to thrive when grown together. Bush beans seem to grow well with beets and cabbages, although they dislike growing near fennel. Medieval gardeners understood the importance of rotating crops – a practice still adopted today – and that growing flowers among vegetables can be highly beneficial. Bees and flies that are attracted to the flowers pollinate beans and fruiting plants, increasing their yield. Pot marigolds (*Calendula officinalis*), with their clear orange or lemon-yellow flowers, confuse whitefly and help tomatoes grow stronger and healthier, while hoverflies destroy harmful pests on brassicas such as cabbages.

To be manageable, a productive garden should be designed with beds that are narrow enough to allow crops to be harvested quickly and easily from a path; this makes routine maintenance practical and prevents compaction of the soil in the beds caused by treading. Paths should be slip-proof; vegetable gardens in the past sometimes had simple paths of cinders from an open fire. If loose materials such as cinders, gravel, or chipped bark are used, they should be edged with wooden shuttering, tiles, or pieces of local stone to prevent them from spilling onto the beds.

In a garden with a fairly formal layout, such as a traditional French-style potager, perhaps with symmetrical beds and a central ornamental feature like a sundial or a large stone urn, substantial, regular paths are more appropriate. These can be of brick laid in a herringbone or basketweave pattern and bordered by terracotta rope edging tiles, or stone, granite, or cobblestones, bedded in cement for stability, depending on the styles and materials favored locally (see also Paths, pages 32–5).

Medieval gardeners understood the importance of rotating crops – a practice still adopted today – and of growing flowers among vegetables.

FAR LEFT *Beet leaves add splashes of rich maroon to a bed of purple and white pansies. Round nasturtium leaves contrast with them, as will their fiery-colored, edible flowers, which make a colorful garnish for sliced beets.*
CENTER *Beans have been allowed to scramble among the bright flowers of pot marigolds (*Calendula officinalis*), which act as a valuable pest repellent in the vegetable patch.*
LEFT *Design in the vegetable garden should involve texture as well as color. Here, an informal path of irregular-shaped white stones bedded in the soil provides easy access to the rows of purple-tinged 'Lollo Rosso' lettuce and orange-flowered nasturtiums.*
FOLLOWING PAGE *Woven hurdles surround this productive flower and vegetable garden. A bower among the beans provides a viewpoint from which to enjoy the plot.*

Functional features

Within the vegetable plot, there is plenty of scope for imaginative touches that are both practical and decorative. Carefully positioned trellis obelisks add height and architectural interest all year round. Not only are they ornamental, they also offer support for climbing vegetables or fruit such as pumpkins or squash, beans or melons. For a less formal look, lash together rough poles or bamboo stakes into wigwams. Twiggy hazel branches make an attractive and effective support for peas or strongly perfumed sweet peas. Traditional terracotta forcing pots, used to blanch seakale or protect early rhubarb, fulfill a valuable function and add an unforced charm in a working part of the garden. Plant old stone urns and troughs with lettuce or leafy vegetables to provide an eccentric appeal.

LEFT *Where space is limited, paths are kept narrow and vegetables that grow vertically, such as peas and beans, are planted.*

ABOVE *Terracotta forcing pots are decorative yet functional. The purple leaves of 'Red Mountain' spinach harmonize with the mauve comfrey. Towering Crambe cordifolia with its dark, textured leaves and airy white flowers provides an ornamental screen at the rear of the patch.*

Growing fruit

ABOVE *Rich ruby clusters of redcurrants hang from standard bushes behind a row of purple lavender. Fruit bushes trained as standards allow plenty of space for underplanting so you can make maximum use of the available ground.*

RIGHT *A screen of trained espaliered apple trees provides a living background for a border of perennials and annuals. Nasturtiums twine themselves up the trees while tall, white-flowered* Nicotiana sylvestris *mingles with feathery-leaved cosmos and, at the front of the border, pink* Cleome hassleriana, *yellow crocosmia, and white dahlias.*

What could be more delightful than to doze in a gently swaying hammock stretched between two ancient apple trees, listening to the drowsy buzz of bees and watching the sun shine on the ripening fruit above? An informal grove or orchard is the ideal way to grow fruit and nut trees if you have the space, especially in a wild garden. Grouping trees together like this improves pollination, which produces a larger harvest as well as making routine cultivation and pruning easier. In temperate regions, apples and pears grow well along with stone fruits such as plums, damsons, and cherries. In Mediterranean countries, gnarled, ancient olive trees, tended by families for generations, bring a sense of continuity to the garden, while groves of orange and lemon trees subtly scent the air.

In a more formal setting, fruit trees can be trained flat against a wall or taut wires stretched between vertical posts into various shapes: fans, cordons (single-stemmed trees often grown diagonally),

Trained fruit trees take up very little space, and the fruit is easily accessible for harvesting.

or espaliers (with tiers of horizontal branches). Trained trees take up very little space and the fruit is easily accessible for harvesting, but the plants generally require more routine maintenance and pruning than free-standing trees. In a very small garden, low "stepover" apple cordons grown on horizontal wires are useful for edging beds of currants, raspberries, or strawberries. Ornamental and productive divisions or screens can be created from fences, trellis panels, or posts and wires covered with trained grapevines, peaches, figs, or currants. In spring, fans and espaliers look particularly attractive covered with blossom, while in summer and fall their evenly spread branches allow the fruit to ripen well, bringing a delicious harvest.

Traditionally, country gardens in temperate areas have often had one or two apple trees. In addition to as being good for eating and versatile in cooking, apples have the advantage that they will store well in a cool place for weeks, even months, to provide fruit for winter without having to be made into preserves. Rowan trees (*Sorbus*) were popular in country areas for their brilliant red berries that could be made into a tart jelly to accompany meat; the fruits of crab apples (*Malus*), which may be bright red or golden-yellow, are used in a similar way. A rowan was once thought to have the power to protect a house and garden from witches, and its wood was used for carvings that were believed to bring good luck.

LEFT *Figs have been grown and valued as food since ancient times. They thrive with restricted root growth, so they are ideal for large pots on terraces where they can be kept pruned to a manageable size.* CENTER *This orange orchard has reached full maturity, and ripe, fallen fruit scatters the earth beneath the laden trees. The scent of the flowers is sweet and heady; even one orange tree grown in a conservatory will perfume the air.* RIGHT *The golden plum 'Thomas Cross' is a wonderful color and easy to grow, but pollination may be poor in a cold spring when there are few bees around.*

The country herb garden

Any plant that has a use – culinary, medicinal, household, or for perfume – may be classified as a herb. Herbs have held an important place in man's life since ancient times: the Chinese were aware of their value over 5,000 years ago; the Egyptians used herbs to embalm their Pharaohs; in Europe, the Greeks crowned winning athletes with coronets of bay and fennel, while the Romans presented noble warriors with garlands of herbs. Country people have long prized the precious qualities of these plants and included them in their gardens as medicines and cure-alls for their families and animals; as strewing herbs to scent the house, deter vermin, and ward off illness; and to add variety and flavor to their food.

For the contemporary gardener, much of the history and folklore attached to herbs is still fascinating, even if some of the traditional beliefs about their properties are now regarded as superstitions. In fact, many herbs are still invaluable in the kitchen for adding flavor to dishes and infusing as tea, in the home to scent linen and guard clothes against moths, and as the basis for many simple natural remedies and beauty preparations. In the garden, although few herbs are showy plants or have large flowers, they offer an enormous range of delicious scents and attractive foliage to enjoy. On a summer's day, heat releases their essential oils, filling the air with heady perfume. To savor the tangy scent of lemon balm, the fresh aroma of peppermint, or the aniseed fragrance of fennel, grow herbs next to a path or around your doorway so that you can crush a leaf or two between your fingers as you pass.

LEFT *The architectural form of angelica adds height to a herb garden, while the gray-blue leaves of a globe artichoke also add structure and textural interest. The chives have been allowed to flower to add color to the plan.*

ABOVE *Delicate fronds of bronze fennel accentuate the different yellows and greens of this herb patch. Yellow pearl-headed tansy makes the airy fennel flowerheads appear more fragile, while the flat, dense, yellow heads of yarrow (Achillea) add depth to the planting.*

Herbs in beds and borders

With such a vast number of herbs available, it is possible to create a garden devoted entirely to herbs, and because many have not been as hybridized as more ornamental plants, they are well suited to the artless charm and relaxed feel of a country garden. Many look good mixed randomly among traditional country garden flowers, such as columbines, astrantia, love-in-a-mist, lupines, and wallflowers, or they can be grown in a patch on their own.

One traditional approach when designing a herb garden is to divide the plants according to use – with separate beds for culinary, medicinal, dyeing, and scented herbs. Roman gardens had a formal skeleton of square or rectangular beds contained by box hedges; these clipped frames kept herbs for different uses distinct, but a much more informal design could be used in a country garden by simply separating beds with lines of stones or cobblestones, or grass paths. In a small garden, a space-saving idea is to make a herb bed within an old wagon wheel laid on the soil or in a circular raised bed – a different herb is grown in each section between the wheel spokes, but with this method it is best to select only those herbs that all enjoy the same conditions and to choose low-growing types for the design to have maximum impact.

Grouping herbs together by their color looks particularly eyecatching; although few herbs have spectacular or brilliant flowers, many have handsome colored or variegated foliage. In one bed, you could grow golden-leaved and yellow-variegated herbs, such as golden thyme (*Thymus caespititius* 'Aureus'), golden marjoram (*Origanum vulgare* 'Aureum' or 'Gold Tip'), golden sage (*Salvia officinalis* 'Kew Gold'), and ginger mint (*Mentha × gracilis* 'Variegata'), which has yellow-splashed leaves; in another, bronze and purple plants – the burnished coppery-bronze fennel (*Foeniculum vulgare* 'Purpureum'), purple sage (*Salvia officinalis* Purpurascens Group), purple basil (*Ocimum basilicum* var. *purpurascens*), lavender (*Lavandula angustifolia*), and the lilac-flowered form of bergamot (*Monarda fistulosa*). A silver- and white-themed bed could include silver thyme (*Thymus vulgaris* 'Silver Posie'), gray cotton lavender (*Santolina chamaecyparissus*), and wormwood (*Artemisia absinthium* 'Lambrook Silver').

Many herbs make delightful additions to flower borders, intermingled with ornamental perennials and shrubs. Lovage (*Levisticum officinale*) and angelica (*Angelica archangelica*) provide tall, architectural clumps that stand proudly amid roses, red valerian, and the large daisy flowers of margaritas. Chives (*Allium schoenoprasum*) make an attractive edging, with their narrow, cylindrical leaves and

Herbs are well suited to the artless charm and relaxed feel of a country garden.

LEFT *This classical herb garden is based on a simple layout. The central path leading to a rose arch is surrounded by a sea of lavender and lady's mantle (*Alchemilla mollis*), with brilliant touches of color provided by geraniums.*
ABOVE *Spikes of pokeweed (*Phytolacca americana*) mixed with fennel add height to this formal, square bed edged with rue (*Ruta graveolens*).*

LEFT *Bunches of fennel seedheads and marjoram are hung up to dry in the sun. Apart from looking decorative, dried perennial herbs such as these are a useful addition to winter meals.*

BELOW *A rustic bench is home to a pot of mixed thymes; here, the gardener can sit and view the garden while crushing the leaves of the thymes to release their scent. Variegated myrtle edges the bed, which is spilling over with nasturtiums, chives, and mallow.*

RIGHT *Purple globe heads of alliums and apricot flowers of* Nectaroscordum siculum *subsp.* bulgaricum *tower above soft mounds of herbs, which are contained within a frame of clipped box.*

pinkish-mauve flowerheads, while thymes (*Thymus*) thread their colorful leaves and tiny flowers through the gaps between paving and over the edges of a path or patio. Comfrey (*Symphytum*) is an excellent plant for a wild garden, with blue, mauve, or cream flowers and mounds of coarse leaves. In the past, its English folk name was knitbone because it was believed to speed healing; it does, in fact, increase cell growth and so help heal wounds and bruises and soothe painful joints. In the garden, comfrey can also be used as a "green manure" – grown on a fallow patch, it is then dug in to improve the soil's fertility.

Although tall, fennel (*Foeniculum vulgare*) has soft, feathery foliage in green or tinged with bronze that allows you to see through to other plants beyond, so it can be planted at the front of a bed to add height. The golden hop (*Humulus lupulus* 'Aureus'), with its glorious acid yellow-green leaves, combines well with other climbers such as honeysuckle or a blue-flowered clematis, or can be grown over an arch to mark the entrance to a herb garden. Bergamot (*Monarda didyma*), with its red flowers and ruby-veined leaves, is another good candidate for the flowerbed; its leaves have been used for centuries as a soothing tea, and it is still used today to give Earl Grey tea its distinctive aroma.

Herbs in containers

By the sixteenth century, country people all over Europe were growing "pot herbs." Clustered around a farmhouse doorway or perched on windowsills, terracotta pots held herbs such as sage, thyme, basil, rosemary, and hyssop to provide sprigs for flavoring sauces, soups, and stews. Summer evenings were scented by pot-grown herbs: lavender, with its mass of purple flowerheads, which could be dried to perfume linen and deter moths; delicate-flowered cilantro, used to flavor bread and vegetables; sage, considered a universal cure and made into tea to improve the memory and brainpower; and pungent rosemary, symbolizing fidelity and remembrance, invaluable in cooking and as a powerful antiseptic.

Even the smallest garden should have space for herbs in containers: place pots of herbs to line a flight of garden steps, use terracotta troughs along a low wall or by a garden seat, or position a formal, clipped bay tree (*Laurus nobilis*) by the front door to give height and structure to a carefree grouping of bright orange pot marigolds (*Calendula officinalis*), white lavender (*Lavandula angustifolia* 'Nana Alba'), and chamomile (*Chamaemelum nobile*) with its fine filigree foliage and small, daisylike flowers.

The flavor of fresh, free-range eggs is far superior to that of their battery-farmed counterparts.

Keeping livestock

Country gardening was originally a matter of self-sufficiency; land was devoted to produce which could be either eaten or sold at the market. Now, while many gardeners relish their fresh, homegrown vegetables, they tend to balk at the thought of keeping livestock. However, birds and other animals such as chickens, ducks, geese, even a goat, add vitality, humor, distinctive sounds, and a quirky character that makes a country garden irresistible.

Chickens roaming freely among rows of vegetables or through the verdant grass of an orchard are a cheering sight. The flavor of fresh, free-range eggs is far superior to that of their battery-farmed counterparts. Another advantage is that chickens keep down insect pests in the garden, a truly traditional form of biological control. Old-fashioned breeds, in particular, have decorative plumage.

Roosters are often especially handsome, and their proud crowing is a characteristically rural sound, but they can be highly territorial and possessive of their hens, which may upset the harmony of your plot. Seek expert advice or consult specialist literature on keeping chickens, including the type, number, and sex of the birds, before you decide which to buy. Hens should be shut up at night to protect them from predators, preferably in a secure henhouse with nesting boxes to discourage them from laying their eggs in out-of-the-way places where they may never be found.

Ducks are trusting and often comical creatures that quickly endear themselves to their owners. If your garden includes a pond or stream, consider keeping a small number of birds. There are many species, some very decorative, and they are charming, even amusing, to watch as they glide across the water or waddle around the garden. A small island in a pond can be furnished with a duck

LEFT *A handsome speckled rooster and hens pick over the grass for insects to eat, thereby reducing the amount of damage done by pests to nearby plants.*

CENTER *Geese forage in a wild patch that is bordered by stout rustic fencing. Such an area or orchard is ideal for geese, who tend to be messy creatures and so not suited to a formal, orderly garden.*

ABOVE *White fantailed doves are the most romantic and decorative of birds to keep, bringing movement and great charm to a garden. A large dovecote will house several pairs, which will live together contentedly.*

house made from a barrel that has had one end removed, making a snug nesting box. As with chickens, ducks should be kept in a secure place at night to protect them.

Large white geese make a striking sight as they strut across a broad stretch of grass, appear suddenly around the corner of a hedge or pick over the gravel on a path. They are justly famous for their vigilance and are useful for deterring burglars. Unfortunately, geese cannot differentiate between friend and foe, so, while you can rely on them to sound the alarm when strangers appear, you should put them in a secure pen if you are expecting guests.

In medieval times and even earlier, dovecotes were not the ornamental fancies of today. They were large, sturdy, utilitarian buildings, designed so that some of the kept pigeons' eggs and young – known as squabs – could be removed for the kitchen. Later, keeping doves and pigeons became more a matter of fashion than food, and now these birds add an unusual decorative element to the garden. Dovecotes are often painted white and can be made to look like miniature houses with pitched roofs or pretty touches such as scalloped edging. White fantailed doves and fancy pigeons are noted more for their handsomeness than their loyalty, so newly purchased birds are usually shut in their home for three weeks until they have become familar with it.

Few people today choose to keep a pig or cow; the goat is now the most favored animal for people who have enough space. Goats' milk is ideal for those allergic to cows' milk and may also be made into delicious cheese, perhaps flavored with garden herbs. A goat must have some type of dry shelter such as a lean-to or abandoned stable, but as long as this is available and you do not mind taking food to the animal, a goat may be kept even without a large grazing area. Contrary to popular belief, goats are often fussy eaters and when in milk will need additional food as well as their usual grass or hay.

Nothing can compare with the sweetness of honey from your own hives. Although beekeeping has declined in popularity in the last 20 years, bees are highly rewarding to keep, and if they are cared for properly, even one or two hives will provide enough honey for all the family, with some to spare. Beekeepers who want honey with a particular taste site their hives near specific plants, in a grove of orange trees for orange blossom honey, for example, or on a hillside swathed in heather. A wildflower meadow or orchard well away from the house is a good spot; the hives should be placed where children and animals will not knock into them and where the bees will not be disturbed by electric hedgetrimmers or lawnmowers. Beekeepers traditionally wear white overalls for the highly practical reason that bees rarely sting anything white.

*Blackberries tumble
over hedges in the fall,
staining your fingers
the color of wine
as you pick them.*

The captured harvest

Searching for wild foods in the hedges, woods, fields, and heaths beyond your country garden is one of the great pleasures of a rural lifestyle. How satisfying it is to walk home carrying a basket brimming with creamy-topped mushrooms, touched with dew, to be fried for breakfast, or beautiful blue-black sloe berries for making delicious sloe gin to sip on cold winter evenings. When gathering any berries, leaves, or fungi from the wild, you must be certain about plant identification, because some species are poisonous but look similar to nontoxic plants. Initially, it is best to forage with someone who is experienced and carry a specialist illustrated guide to increase your knowledge as you go. If you are in any doubt about a plant's identity, err on the side of caution and do not pick it.

A country walk may turn up such treasures as tiny wild strawberries in early summer, especially at the edges of woodland, while fall is the best time for harvesting other berries. Then, blackberries tumble over hedges, staining your fingers the color of wine as you pick them. They make a delectable addition to apple pies or can be made into sherbet, ice-cream, and preserves.

By mid-autumn, other berries and fruits are waiting to be gathered. Rowan berries hang in rich scarlet clusters, and shiny golden and red crab apples look wonderfully tempting, ready to be turned into clear jellies to accompany meat dishes. Rosehips, rich in vitamin C, should be pressed and made into syrup soon after being plucked from their briars if they are not to lose their potency; the hips can also be made into soup or wine.

Elder trees are especially worth seeking out, for both the flowers and fruit can be used. In late spring or early summer, pick the creamy flowerheads, which can be made into a delicious sherbet with the delicate flavor of muscatel wine. Alternatively, the heads can be dipped in batter and quickly fried and dusted with powdered sugar for an unusual dessert. The flowers are also made into a nonalcoholic drink known as elderflower "champagne," which is commercially produced in some countries, while the berries make a good, rich wine. Combine the berries with apples for a scrumptious jelly especially loved by children, or with gooseberries to make a syrup. Other fruits such as bilberries, blueberries, huckleberries, damsons, and the small French plums known as myrtilles make excellent pies, jams, and preserves.

LEFT *Blueberries hang in rich, clouded blue clusters. Similar to the northern European bilberry, both types should only be picked once fully ripe, when the berries pull away easily from the cluster.*
CENTER *Hawthorn and sloe berries are often found growing wild together. Sloes have been used to make sloe gin for hundreds of years, while hawthorn berries were once stewed and eaten in times when food was scarce.*
ABOVE *Rosehips and blackberries ripen side by side in a country hedge. Blackberries can be eaten raw or cooked or made into a rich, dark jam or jelly. Rosehips were traditionally made into a syrup, which was taken during the fruitless winter months to guard against colds.*

Herbs, nuts, and fungi

There are many herbs growing in the wild that can be gathered for use in the kitchen. Wild sorrel may be picked to use in sauces or a few of the young leaves added to a green salad for their distinctive tang. Wild thyme, mint, and marjoram are less decorative than the garden varieties, but their flavor is just as good. Pick the young leaves of stinging nettles – wearing gloves, of course – early in the season for cooking in the same way as spinach or for making into soup; avoid nettles after early summer because the older leaves act as a purgative. Dandelion is much maligned as a garden weed, but the young leaves are excellent if lightly blanched and added to a salad; the roots can also be dug up and then roasted and ground to make into a drink rather like coffee.

Gathering nuts is an enjoyable pastime for a fall afternoon, with leaves rustling underfoot as sunshine breaks through the tree canopy. Sweet chestnuts are traditionally roasted on an open fire at Christmas, but they can also be made into a sustaining soup or ground for flour to be used in cakes and pastries. Acorns have been collected in Europe to make a coffee-type beverage and were used by Native Americans, although they are less favored today. Filberts are excellent for candy, cakes, and cookies, as well as for making into a liqueur, but look for them before they are fully ripe because they are also prized by squirrels and other rodents.

Fungi may be found in all seasons of the year, but fall is usually considered the best time. Some species grow in open fields, others in woodland; beech woods are often a particularly good source. You must be sure that you can differentiate between species; although few are highly poisonous, they do resemble some edible types. To pick fungi, twist them gently, including the whole stalk. Place them in an open basket or paper bag rather than a plastic bag; they soon decay if kept sealed in.

Besides the well-known, and much sought-after, ceps (*Boletus edulis*), chanterelles (*Cantharellus cibarius*), and the sadly elusive truffles (*Tuber melanosporum*), there are many other fungi that make tasty meals. There are delicious morels (*Morchella esculenta*), pale oyster mushrooms (*Pleurotus ostreatus*), white field mushrooms (*Agaricus campestris*), and the wonderfully named horn of plenty (*Craterellus cornucopoides*), shaped like a funnel. Most can be cooked and eaten fresh or preserved for later use by drying or pickling. Some are delicious in soups or stews, while others are good enough to be enjoyed almost on their own, perhaps stuffed and served whole, in a sauce as part of a risotto or pasta dish, or simply sautéed and served with scrambled eggs.

LEFT *The heads of sunflowers have been gathered and left to dry in the sun. Their seeds may be cracked open and the kernels eaten as they are, or they can be used in breadmaking.*
ABOVE *Wood blewits (*Lepista nuda*) appear in late autumn; they are one of the most delicious of fungi, but some people can be allergic to them, so it is wise to sample only a tiny piece at first.*
RIGHT *Beside a richly colored pumpkin, Spanish or sweet chestnuts poke out from their porcupinelike shells. They are particularly delicious roasted over an open fire on a winter's night.*

Perfect FURNISHINGS

*A*T THE END OF A LONG, HARD DAY, what could be better than to enjoy the evening air seated on your favorite garden chair, or to gather around a simple trestle table with friends for a relaxed meal and easy conversation? The right garden furniture, positioned in the best spot, can add greatly to the mood and style of a garden. Well-chosen ornaments and planted containers also have a part to play, bringing character and individuality and a personal touch as well as year-round interest. The pleasures of a water feature such as a pond or stream cannot be overestimated – water adds vitality and sound, and attracts a great variety of wildlife. Detail is important in a country garden; small touches catch the eye, create a relaxing atmosphere and contribute to the feeling of rightness. Worn garden tools left casually by the back door or a battered tin watering can laid by a path suggest a sense of continuity and work-in-progress, and capture a moment of peace and stillness in a busy world.

LEFT *An unobtrusively painted table and chairs under a canopy of climbing roses create a harmonious and unforced composition.*

ABOVE *A nineteenth-century Italian marble bath has been made into an attractive water feature, adding a timeless dignity to a shady corner. The wide, mellow stone steps are in keeping with its classical lines and simplicity.*

Choosing garden furniture

Before electricity was introduced to rural areas, many household tasks were performed immediately outside the house to take advantage of daylight. A simple plank bench provided a place to sit while wool was spun, clothes mended, and vegetables prepared for cooking. Stone benches in the shade of a house wall are still common features in the Mediterranean, tempting the gardener to rest. A patio or terrace furnished with comfortable chairs and a large table becomes an outdoor room where family get-togethers can take place in the fresh air, perhaps shaded from the sun's heat by a tree or a pergola and surrounded by sweet-smelling plants.

If you want permanent furniture in the garden, carefully consider its position. The natural choice is usually a spot that takes advantage of a good view, either onto a broad outlook, such as a distant hill, or some small-scale yet no less pleasing feature – a rush-fringed pond, a particularly fine rose, a bed of scented herbs. A garden seat becomes a feature in its own right, so first try placing an indoor chair in different locations around the garden. This can help you judge how a seat might alter the mood and balance of each area and to see what part it plays in the design from different angles and viewpoints. Think about the practical function of the furniture, too; do you want

LEFT *During long, dry summers, chairs from the house can be left out for days around a sturdy table in the cool shade of a tree. Food seems to have more flavor when eaten in the balmy air with birds and crickets singing nearby.*

BELOW *An unassuming wooden bench is set in a wild garden, providing a strong focal point as well as a spot from which to enjoy the scene's tranquility. Ox-eye daisies spangle the long grass as they nod in the gentle breeze.*

BELOW *A painted wicker chair under a small tree provides the perfect retreat for daydreaming. Thousands of buttercups glow among lush grass, creating an oasis of uncultivated splendor.*

RIGHT *An ornate iron and wooden bench adds a sophisticated touch and formal structure that complement the deep herbaceous borders. A vigorous rambling rose cascades from a large tree, creating an airy, romantic mood.*

a seat away from the house that offers peace and solitude, a group of chairs for social occasions, or both? If the seating area is in full sun, you may also need to consider providing some shade.

Even in regions where the weather is variable or inclement, permanent stone or treated wooden furniture has an important ornamental role to play; it also saves wasting precious time hunting for chairs should there be a brief break in the clouds. A circular or hexagonal wooden seat built around the trunk of a large tree offers a delightful place to relax beneath the spreading branches and gaze across the garden. A seat can be built into a high stone or brick wall, creating a sheltered spot from where you can appreciate the garden even on a windy day. It could also double as a ledge for containers of evergreen shrubs during the winter months.

You may prefer to have light folding tables and chairs so you can move them to different areas of the garden according to your mood and the occasion. A plain slatted wooden table with wood and canvas director's chairs are both attractive and portable, while

traditional striped deckchairs add a leisurely look and are particularly appropriate in coastal gardens. A hammock attached between two sturdy trees or other strong supports is perfect for relaxing on a balmy summer's day. There are simple types made of fine rope mesh or more elaborate woven versions which are often available in a wide choice of colors and patterns.

Whether it is a simple plank bench, an ornate wrought-iron table and chairs, or a chic wooden lounger, the outdoor furniture you choose helps to create the overall garden picture. Look for furniture that will harmonize with the other design elements, rather than be too dominant or obtrusive. Coastal plots enclosed with lichen-encrusted stone walls would suggest very plain, unpretentious pieces. Rustic tables and chairs buffeted by salt-laden sea air take on a weathered, well-used look that blends well with the garden's surroundings. Where summers are long and dry, fabric-covered deckchairs and swing benches with canopies can be left in place from one day to the next to become bleached by the sun.

ABOVE *A hammock slung beneath the boughs of a tree offers a shady resting place from which to appreciate the pale flowers of sweet rocket, columbines, wallflowers, and rock roses growing among purple-blue veronica.*

FOLLOWING PAGE *The weathered iron table and chairs blend in perfectly with the wild, uncultivated look of this country garden. Red valerian and weigela glow in the soft evening light.*

*Soft blues, grays,
and greens blend in
with the garden,
offering subtle shifts in
tone and hue, while
strong colors draw the
eye immediately.*

A more formal country garden, perhaps with clipped box edging and topiary, calls for more refined seating. Heavy hardwood seats with slatted backs look at home among standard roses and tumbling clematis; they are available in a wide choice of designs, such as latticework, chinoisierie, and the classic, to suit your taste and the ambience of the garden. Chairs of wrought-iron or more lightweight alloys have the advantage of allowing plants and views to be glimpsed through them. They are usually painted or otherwise treated to protect them from corrosion; some have ornate designs such as intertwining leaves and flowers, while others are understated, with a plain gothic-arched back or vertical spars.

With the careful addition of color, an ordinary wooden chair can become a striking feature. Soft blues, grays, and greens blend in

with the garden, offering subtle shifts in tone and hue, while strong colors draw the eye immediately. In cool regions where the flowering season is relatively short, introduce colored chairs and tables to enliven the garden. The muted, natural tones of a rough stone wall or old shed roofed with rusty corrugated iron can be offset to dramatic effect by positioning a bench of vivid emerald green or tomato red nearby. Paintwork that is distressed or peeling makes an artificial object such as a chair or table look more natural, as if it had sprung up with the rest of the garden. For a more formal look, you may prefer the pristine appearance of a fresh coat of paint. The fabric for chair seat cushions may be chosen in colors that harmonize with adjacent plants; alternatively, they can be in sharp contrast to the plants to introduce an element of surprise.

LEFT *The painted chair is a key component in the color scheme of this verdant garden as it picks up the color of the phlox behind.*
CENTER *A quiet seating area is enlivened by the introduction of a red-and-white-striped deckchair.*
ABOVE *Dense, informal planting has created a country atmosphere in this town garden. The red leaves of the amelanchier are a striking contrast to the soft green painted table and chair, which merge into their surroundings.*

ABOVE *A stone pillar sundial acts as an anchor and focal point for this area of a garden. Its strong, clear shape contrasts with the haphazard leaf growth of the pumpkins that surround it.*

RIGHT *Even a mailbox can be an amusing and ornamental addition to a garden. At first sight, this looks like a birdhouse, but the holes in it are too narrow, and no bird would choose such an exposed home.*

Country garden ornaments

Ornamental features provide focal points or surprises in the garden, help create a particular style and atmosphere, and add structural interest. They also give clues to the personality and imagination of the gardener, allowing touches of individual expression. In a rural garden, ornaments can evoke another age and establish a line of continuity between past and present. A worn cart wheel propped against the wall of an old stable or potting shed recalls days when the horse was more important than the car, and transportation operated at a more leisurely pace than it does today.

It is worth taking time and trouble to find the most suitable ornaments for your site. The design, scale, and materials of any piece should be in keeping with the style of the garden so it looks at home. A neoclassical figure might look too formal in full view in a small country garden, for example, but could be perfect half-hidden among ferns. Keep a lookout for interesting pieces in architectural salvage and junk yards and at country auctions. Consider whether an ornament will be best seen as an important focal point, perhaps at the end of a flower-edged path or against the dark background of a box hedge, or placed in a less obvious position so that visitors come across it almost by chance and can enjoy their secret discovery. Use the style and layout of the garden and the materials and characteristics of the local landscape to inspire you.

A sundial mounted on a stone pedestal makes a strong focal point; it could be set in the center of a formal rose garden or traditional vegetable patch to act as the lynchpin around which the whole area is planted. Surrounded by billowing bushes of white and pink roses and underplanted with lavender, a sundial suggests an element of order and regularity amid the abundance of plants.

Birdbaths are ornamental as well as beneficial to bird life and bird lovers, and any shallow, water-filled container of a reasonable size placed near shrubs will always attract birds. Ornate stone birdbaths raised on a pedestal or plinth will add height to a bed of low-growing plants and allow birds to bathe and drink safely out of the reach of any cats. Large, colored, glazed plant saucers filled with water will attract birds; placed on a paved area, they reflect the sky and introduce an unexpected splash of color.

Staddle stones are distinctive features for a country garden, with an unpretentious, rustic look. Shaped like stone mushrooms, they were originally used to support wooden grain bins, because they were difficult for rodents to climb. Positioned toward the end of a flowerbed, a staddle stone arrests the eye and focuses attention on the freer forms of the plants around it. Site a pair on each side of a

gate or path to mark an entrance. In agricultural regions, the walls of brick buildings appear more interesting decorated with an array of old ironwork and horse tackle such as pieces of bridles, harnesses, and horseshoes. Traditionally, a horseshoe was nailed above a doorway to bring good luck, and it was believed that if the horseshoe slipped so that the ends pointed downward, the owner's luck would run out.

Statues have been used to decorate gardens since ancient times. The Romans placed figures of their gods in their gardens, and even now a corner with a statue surrounded by plants almost has the air of a shrine. Small, well-worn statues, or even broken fragments of a figure, suit rural gardens. A chipped Greek priestess's head set under a tree surrounded by wild plants and grass adds a human touch amid the abstract forms and shapes of plants. A stone frog peeping out from behind hosta leaves introduces an element of surprise and complements the shape and texture of the foliage.

Architectural stone features, such as spheres, pillars, and cubes, contribute strong geometric shapes and a sense of solidity and structure that sits well alongside wild plants, or they can echo the distinctive silhouettes of topiary. A stone sphere could be positioned at the front of a bed so the plants surround it like a living frame, or at the foot of a flight of steps as a punctuation point. A stone pillar or obelisk draws the eye to a particular part of the garden and provides vertical interest all year round (see also Plant Supports, pages 127–31).

Wall plaques with low-relief designs or scenes and decorative masks are usually made out of reconstituted stone or terracotta, although wooden masks can also be treated with preservative and hung on a garden wall. Mounted on a stone wall and half-covered with ivy and clematis, a plaque gives additional impact to a simple planting. For a unique feature, you could design a mosaic to create a picture or geometric pattern, perhaps one that mimics the distinctive forms of nearby plants; mosaic tiles can be laid flat on the ground or cemented onto a wall.

Rural plots that include areas of long grass, informally planted areas, woodland, or coastal dunes may call for ornamental features that look natural rather than man-made. Objects such as moss-encrusted tree branches or trunks, irregular pieces of stone, large mottled pebbles and cobblestones, and shells or driftwood provide interesting textures and forms shaped by nature. In dappled shade, the small, delicate flowers of cyclamen look appealing nestling among carefully placed, lichen-covered tree branches. A decaying tree trunk makes a handsome backcloth for clear yellow primroses and starry-flowered *Anemone blanda*.

LEFT *A stone-colored dish acts as a birdbath, the water reflecting the sky and plants above. Its quiet color harmonizes with the subtle shades of the Shirley poppies (*Papaver rhoeas*), which flower freely around it.*

ABOVE *Painted a muted cream, pink, and green, a birdhouse is tucked almost out of sight among the foliage, offering a safe nesting site for a small bird.*

RIGHT *A staddle stone sits snugly among the scented Hybrid Musk rose 'Penelope,'* Sisyrinchium striatum, *and the gray leaves of lambs' ears (*Stachys byzantina*), its rough texture and distinctive shape contrasting well with the softness of the plants.*

Architectural features contribute a sense of solidity and structure that sits well alongside wild plants.

LEFT *A double arch above a low picket gate provides an attractive support for beans. A weatherproof lantern hangs from the arch and is lit at night to guide and welcome visitors.*

ABOVE *An old chimney, blackened with age, adds an original touch and a solid focal point in a bed thickly planted with* Allium aflatunense, Sisyrinchium striatum, *red valerian, and a long-flowering geranium.*

Country containers

There is an endless variety of containers to buy – tubs and pots, barrels and buckets, sinks and troughs – and with a little imagination, many other types of vessel can be adapted to hold plants or function as ornaments in their own right. Containers have been used in gardens since Roman times, and many of the styles that are familiar today have changed little since then. They provide architectural interest and are highly versatile design elements: they can be moved around to bring additional color to an area, act as a focal point, or be easily be replanted if you wish to change the display. In plots with poor soil, they allow the gardener to grow a greater variety of plants, and they are ideal for growing tender plants in cool climates because they can be brought in to shelter for winter.

Plain pots and tubs act as foils for more elaborate planting, and they can be used in groups without looking too fussy. Unadorned terracotta pots planted with herbs can be lined up on a low garden

BELOW *A pot with flaking paint makes a good marriage with the variegated leaves of an overflowing glechoma and a euonymus on the right. The casual mood is enhanced by the free-flowering campanula and roses behind.*

wall or kitchen windowsill so that you have access to the herbs and can easily tend them. Cluster pots around the back door to bring the garden almost into the house or place troughs or tubs packed with plants beside a front gate or walk for a welcoming sight.

Choose containers that fit the style and atmosphere of your garden. In addition to wooden half-barrels and square planters, clay pots and basins, stone urns and troughs, you may also come across containers made of reconstituted stone, fiberglass resin, and heavy-duty plastic. Although they are less expensive and often more lightweight than those in natural materials, they tend not to mellow with age and may look inappropriate in a country setting; trailing plants that tumble over the sides will help to offset this.

Half-barrels will give good service for many years and, if left unpainted, have a natural, rustic appeal. As they are heavy, try them in various positions before filling them with potting mix. Terracotta pots are available in a wide choice of styles and with different decorations such as swags, garlands, or basketweave patterns. Some

pots are vulnerable to frost damage; in cold regions, reduce the risk of cracking by raising them off the ground on bricks or matching terracotta "feet" designed for this purpose.

Plant containers can be improvised from large tins, buckets, and baskets, stone sinks, beer and sherry barrels, chimney, wooden vegetable boxes, and animal troughs. Excess water must be able to drain away, so make drainage holes in the base if necessary. A stone sink is perfect for creating a miniature garden. Tiny-leaved plants that would be dwarfed and overwhelmed by hefty neighbors in a bed will thrive in a sink, which forms a plain frame to offset them. Grow pretty *Sisyrinchium bellum*, with its iris-like leaves and blue flowers, alongside miniature pinks (*Dianthus*) and phlox.

Long, wooden animal troughs make unusual containers that look good in a semi-wild setting. Troughs originally used for duck or chicken feed are low, so they are suitable for one side of a terrace where they will not obstruct views out to the rest of the garden. Deeper troughs, formerly used to hold food for cattle, pigs, or sheep, are sometimes made of metal or even stone. They are heavy, and so should be sited in a permanent position.

Chimneys are ideal for trailing plants and for adding height to a group of tubs or pots. Builders' yards stock chimneys of different heights, or you may unearth unusual old ones in salvage yards – square pots, for example, or those with ornamental detailing such as a piecrust finish or patterns stamped into the clay. Grow plants in a separate flowerpot and then place it in the top of the chimney; you can then change the planting quickly and easily if you want to create a different look.

A plant-filled basket laid on a table or on an old wooden chair has an unaffected charm. Baskets add textural interest and may also be painted so they complement garden furniture or form a foil for a particular plant. They are not very durable, however, and should be coated with polyurethane varnish or paint to extend their life. Place plants in flowerpots first, then group them in the basket, removing and replacing them when necessary.

A bare wall can be made more exciting by mounting one or two containers on it in strategic positions; this is a particularly good way of growing plants whose beauty is best seen close up, because you can scrutinize them at eye level. There are wall pots shaped like heads – one of these would look appealing planted with snowdrops, which could spill over to fringe the eyes, and offset by a backcloth of variegated ivy. An iron hay manger makes a sizable wall planter, and it immediately adds a rural atmosphere to a garden if it is attached to a barn or shed. It needs to be lined to retain soil – for this you could use black plastic disguised with a covering of straw.

Plant supports

Clothed in rambling roses, scented summer jasmine, or sky-blue morning glory, a pergola or arch can be a delightful feature in a country garden. In addition to introducing an architectural focal point, these structures provide support for climbing plants and can be used to frame a view or walkway, or link one area of the garden with another. Pergolas have been popular since at least as early as Roman times, when vine-covered structures offered a welcome shady retreat under their leafy canopies in the hot Mediterranean climate. Arbors – ornate, open structures made of wood, wrought iron, or fancy wirework – were especially popular in the eighteenth and nineteenth centuries; they were usually covered in roses and had open sides to let in the scent of the blooms.

Lutyens-style pergolas are constructed with sturdy brick or square stone pillars and strong cross-beams, cut at an angle at the ends; these are durable and provide a reliable support for heavy plants such as laburnum or wisteria. Lighter structures can be made from

LEFT *From the fragrant coolness of a trellised arbor covered with roses, the view along this path sweeps toward an intriguing doorway in a wall which also bears a climbing rose. Heavy climbers need strong structures such as these for support if they are to flourish.*

ABOVE *This sturdy pergola allows a profusely flowering honeysuckle to run riot over its beams while a flamboyant pink rose clambers up its side. Both plants are heavily scented to make strolling or resting beneath the pergola a sensuous delight.*

An ornamental support provides a focal point while surrounding plants are becoming established, and adds contrasting height and structure.

LEFT *A traditional arrangement of stakes provides structural interest and a support for beans. The hedge of* Rosa gallica *'Versicolor' in the foreground has been pruned low to keep its stems self-supporting.*

ABOVE *Old, rusting springs anchored to poles set among fading daylilies* (Hemerocallis) *make idiosyncratic features in their own right and could support a forest of climbing nasturtiums.*

RIGHT *A beautiful twig cage of prunings has been constructed over a sea holly* (Eryngium) *to give support to its lax late-flowering stems. The cage contrasts well with the formal urn, while its color complements the marjoram.*

strong wooden uprights combined with trellis panels for the roof; you can also add trellis at the sides to offer a foothold for a range of climbing and scrambling plants while still allowing leaf-fringed views of the garden beyond.

Much of the appeal of country flowerbeds lies in their untamed look, with plants spilling onto paving, enveloping a wall, or cascading over a trellis. Certain plants must be supported, however, if the whole effect is not to slide from haphazard charm into unkempt chaos. One approach is to use unobtrusive supports, such as twiggy branches known as pea sticks, or posts and wires that will be partly hidden once the plants have grown up. Alternatively, you can use supports that are as decorative as the plants themselves.

Not only does an ornamental support provide a focal point while the surrounding plants are becoming established, it also offers year-round interest, which is useful if you are growing deciduous climbers. Supports may be used to create contrasting height and structure in a bed of low-growing plants or as distinctive markers to accentuate the lines of a design – at the four corners of a vegetable plot, for example, or in the center of a symmetrical herb garden. Even quite a formal feature such as a stone pillar may be effective in an informal context, counterpointing the looser forms of the plants.

The strong, geometric shape of an old stone obelisk topped with a ball finial makes a striking addition to any garden. Antique and reproduction metal obelisks, which are made of iron or steel and then painted, are also available. Wooden obelisks and tripods with trellis sides first became popular in the seventeenth century; they have a lighter, more delicate appearance than those made of stone and may look more appropriate for country gardens. They are often painted white, but this color can be obtrusive; for a softer look, use dark green, grayish-blue, or lavender.

Rustic poles formed into a wigwam have a much simpler, more informal effect. They provide a sturdy support which will take the weight of a combination of climbers such as a rose and clematis or a wisteria. Bamboo stakes are suitable for more lightweight plants

such as sweet peas or morning glory. To prevent plants from flopping onto a path or lawn, you can edge a border with miniature rustic hurdles; they can be moved to a new spot as the need arises. Made of split chestnut, they wear well with age and should last many years.

The art of treillage – making latticework out of wooden struts or strips – has been practiced since at least as long ago as the fourteenth century. The fashion peaked in France in the late seventeenth century when elaborate structures were made which echoed the architectural forms and details of solid buildings. Now trellis is widely available ready-made in sheets of all shapes and sizes, including trompe l'oeil designs that mimic the look of an arch tunnel in perspective. Lightweight trellis, usually of a diamond or square pattern, is often mounted on a wall to provide a support for climbing plants. Sturdier versions, supported by posts set in concrete, can be made into screens to divide the garden, creating separate areas while still retaining an airy, open feel and allowing seductive glimpses of what lies beyond.

LEFT *Roses, threaded through wires, climb these neoclassical pillars to create a blanket of flowers. Foxgloves have sown themselves among the roses, adding a contrast of form while complementing their color.*

CENTER *A window has been created in a wall of rustic trelliswork neatly overlaid with wires to support sweet peas. In the vegetable garden beyond, a willow cone protects seedlings from accidental trampling.*

RIGHT *A painted obelisk brings out the colors of this thoughtfully planned border while providing a climbing frame for a clematis growing alongside the foxgloves and a polygonum.*

Water features

A pond or stream adds a feeling of life and movement to a garden and creates a harmony with the natural rhythms of the countryside. How relaxing it is to sit beside tranquil waters and watch emerald-green dragonflies dip and dart across the surface; on a hot day, just the sound of a trickling stream or bubbling fountain is soothing and cooling. Water features allow you to grow a greater variety of plants and also attract wildlife such as water birds, newts, and frogs, which are fascinating to watch and help to keep down the slug population.

Perhaps you are lucky enough to have a natural pond on your land, fed by springs that keep the water fresh. A farm pond overgrown at the edges with yellow iris and rushes, even cluttered with broken terracotta drainage pipes, has a unique charm and becomes a haven for butterflies, amphibians, and birds as well as home to domestic ducks and geese. To the plantsman, a natural pond is a great blessing, offering the conditions to grow a wonderful selection of plants. Huge rhubarblike *Gunnera manicata* or rodgersias planted at the pond's damp margin turn it into a lush jungle. Candelabra primulas (such as *Primula bulleyana*) in pale pink, cerise-red, or orange massed thickly among long grass and ferns are an arresting sight.

LEFT *A large country pond reflects the light and provides a foil for the upright forms of the naturalistic planting surrounding it. The tall, dark-leaved mountain spinach echoes the spikes of white mullein (*Verbascum*), while yellow evening primrose (*Oenothera*) adds balance to the planting.*

ABOVE *Water gardens can be an exciting jungle of growth. Here, the large leaves of ornamental rhubarb (*Rheum palmatum 'Atrosanguineum'*) grow close to the pond. A silvery willow adds variety of form and color, as does the small metal grasshopper.*

You can design a pond to look like part of a stream by making it long and narrow in places; stepping stones or a simple footbridge across it complete the illusion.

LEFT *Frogs (and toads) are a welcome addition to any garden, helping to keep it free from slugs and other small pests.*
CENTER *A tranquil, tree-ringed lake glistens in the sunlight, making this an idyllic spot in which to relax. The wooden jetty, edged with purple loosestrife, acts as both seating area and viewing platform, while the benches frame the view of the lake beyond.*

Even the tiniest garden has room for a pool: a sunken half-barrel will mirror the sky and is deep enough for a waterlily (*Nymphaea*) and an iris. By placing a piece of wood at an angle in the water, frogs and other small creatures can climb out. To prevent the water from becoming stagnant, a small fountain can be installed to oxygenate and circulate the water. Larger artificial ponds are best made with a flexible liner such as butyl rubber; this allows you to create a naturalistic shape and the material withstands severely cold weather more reliably than concrete or rigid preformed ponds. The edge of the lining can be concealed by stone paving in a terrace, tucked under the sod if in a lawn, or extended under soil in a wild patch to make a damp area for bog plants. You can design a pond to look like

part of a stream by making it long and narrow. Position boulders at one end to create the impression that its source lies beneath them, and place stepping stones or a simple plank footbridge across it to complete the illusion. A planting of willows (*Salix*) or maples (*Acer*) could overhang and disguise the far end.

In a garden with no natural water, the sound and pleasure of a spring can be recreated by installing a millstone or bubble fountain, with water gently running over the millstone or splashing onto cobblestones or pebbles set on a grid above a small reservoir with a pump. You can make such a feature appear more natural by growing plants such as hostas, ferns, and ornamental grasses around it and by letting creeping plants edge onto the stones.

An elegant pedestal fountain gently spills
water into the pool at its feet. The sound
of running water is both calming and
soothing; in ancient times, it was
considered a vital element in the gardens
of the Mediterranean and Middle East.
The exuberant planting of acanthus
and roses offsets the formal style of the
fountain and creates a feeling of lushness.

Tools of the trade

Ancient implements such as a rusting garden roller or a
wheelbarrow left under a gnarled apple tree, or a weathered
wooden rake casually propped against the wall of a shed, give the
impression that generations of gardeners have tended the plot,
offering a comforting thread of continuity and timelessness.
Traditional metal tools with wooden handles, preferably old ones
that have been smoothed and burnished through years of use, are
pleasing to look at and hold as well as being very practical.
Likewise, an old-fashioned wooden water barrel is decorative and
also useful. With its gently curving sides and wooden lid, it makes a
soothing focal point, especially if a traditional basket made from
stripped willow is perched on top.

*Ancient implements
give the impression
that generations of
gardeners have tended
the plot, offering a
thread of continuity
and timelessness.*

FAR LEFT *This beautiful old apple
tree cascading with mistletoe makes a
fitting backcloth for a heavy lawn roller,
speckled with rust.*

LEFT *In the cool darkness of this tool
shed, the gardener has all the implements
on hand for every type of task. The
various forks each have their own
function, and the galvanized wire is used
for training climbing plants and shrubs.*

BELOW *The thick rubber tire of this wheelbarrow means no damage will be caused to the lawn. The long-handled fork is invaluable for turning the soil at the back of a thickly planted bed.*
RIGHT *An antique, galvanized metal water carrier rests among a clump of variegated periwinkles (*Vinca*). Although the statuesque euphorbia grows well in such a dry spot, the pots of pansies will need daily watering.*

In the nineteenth century, galvanized watering cans were produced in many sizes, with different sprinklers so the gardener could water plants correctly, according to their needs. They are as useful today as they were a hundred years ago, and if you have not inherited one, they can still be found in secondhand stores and at auctions.

A well-organized tool shed makes a pleasant and productive workplace. Tools are neatly arranged around the sides of the shed, each with its own allotted space. Stainless steel blades gleam like new, wiped clean before they are put away, and ancient wooden dibbers lie ready to be used alongside rows of carefully cleaned clay pots, all diligently graded by size. There may be stacks of folded

burlap bags that will serve to protect tender plants through biting winds and frosts. Torn into strips, they can be wound around the stems of standard roses to save them from being frozen solid.

Glass bell jars or hand lights placed over special seedlings look like extraordinary flowers sprung up from the earth, and small glass cloches have an ageless appeal. Hand lights of different shapes and sizes were in use by the mid-eighteenth century to protect young and tender plants from frost. Garden frames and cloches made of wood and glass have been in use even longer, since the early seventeenth century, proving that a well-designed garden implement never goes out of fashion.

Beautiful glass cloches, as charming as they are practical, protect newly planted tender subjects from late overnight frosts and from being eaten by slugs and snails.

Index

Author's Acknowledgments

I would like to thank Rosie Atkins for my first commission; Stuart Cooper for having confidence in me; and Helen Ridge, Julia Pashley and Sue Storey who made my ideas come alive.

Publisher's Acknowledgments

The publisher would like to thank the following photographers and organizations for their kind permission to reproduce the photographs in this book.

1 Andrew Lawson (Eastgrove Cottage Garden Nursery, Hereford & Worcester); 2-3 Richard Felber; 4-5 World of Interiors (Simon Upton); 6 Brigitte Perdereau; 7 Beatrice Pichon-Clarisse (Wy-dit-Joli Village); 8 left Ken Druse; 8-9 Jerry Harpur (Bruno Goris-Ponce, Alpes-Maritimes, France); 10 left Roger Foley (Longview Farm/Joanna Reed); 10-11 John de Visser (Feir Mill); 12-13 Christian Sarramon (Maria Hofker); 13 below Campagne, Campagne (Mouchy); 13 top Jacqui Hurst (Lavenham Priory, Suffolk); 14-15 Richard Felber (Newport, Rhode Island); 15 Roger Foley (Colonial Williamsburg); 16-17 Marianne Majerus (Elsing Hall, Norfolk); 18 Richard Felber (Michael Trap, Cornwall, Connecticut); 19 Peter Woloszynski/The Interior Archive; 20-1 Richard Felber; 20 left Marijke Heuff (Rietbrinkhof); 21 right Andrew Lawson (Vann, Surrey); 22-3 Naturbild (Kenneth Bengtsson); 24 left Deidi von Schaewen (Priere d'Orsan à Mowponnais, France); 24-5 Simon Mc Bride (Landriana Garden, Rome); 25 right S & O Mathews; 26-7 Brigitte Perdereau (Chaumont S/Loire); 28 The Garden Picture Library (Jerry Pavia); 29 J C Mayer - G Le Scanff (Festival des Jardins de Chaumont-Sur-Loire, France/Simone Kroll); 30 Brigitte Perdereau (Niccolo Grassi); 31 Richard Felber (Brian Stoner, Cold Springs, Arkansas); 32-3 Richard Felber (Cape Cod, Massachusetts); 32 left Andrew Lawson (Designer: Ryl Nowell, Cabbages & Kings, Wilderness Farm); 33 right Christian Sarramon; 34 left Dency Kane (Dean Riddle Garden, Lanesville, NY); 34-5 Dency Kane (Jacobs/White Garden, East Hampton, NY); 36 Simon McBride (Iford Manor, Wiltshire); 37 top Andrew Lawson (The Old Chapel, Chalford); 37 below Christian Sarramon (Maison Decougne, Wirtz); 38 Richard Felber; 39 Sunniva Harte (Frith Lodge, Mr & Mrs G. Cridland); 40-1 Ivan Terestchenko ('The Garden Room', Clarkson N Potter); 41 right Jessie Walker (Van Valin); 42-3 Brigitte Perdereau (Woodhouse Sussex); 42 left S & O Mathews (Furzey, Hampshire); 43 right Juliette Wade (Peter & Susy Farrell, Woodnewton, Northants); 44-5 Brigitte Perdereau; 45 Sunniva Harte (Frith Lodge, Mr & Mrs G. Cridland); 46 left Richard Felber; 46-7 Jerry Harpur (Deborah Kellaway, Waveney Rising, Norfolk); 47 right Andrew Lawson (Chilcombe House, Dorset); 48-9 Richard Felber (Oehme van Sweden); 49 right Jerry Harpur (Marguerite McBey, Tangier, Morocco); 50-1 Andrew Lawson (Designer: Anthony Archer-Wills); 50 left Inside/V. Motte; 51 right Andrew Lawson; 52 left Jacqui Hurst (Wretham Lodge, Norfolk); 52-3 Andrew Lawson (Sticky Wicket, Buckland Newton, Dorset); 54-5 S & O Mathews (12 Rozelle Close, Littleton, Hampshire); 55 top Gary Rogers (Erika Jahnke); 55 below S & O Mathews; 56 left Michael Busselle; 56-7 Jerry Harpur (The Manor House, Bledlow, Bucks); 57 below Marcus Harpur; 58 Juliette Wade (Dr & Mrs Cox, Woodpeckers, Warwickshire); 59 Christian Sarramon (Wirtz); 60 S & O Mathews; 61 Michael Busselle; 62 left Andrew Lawson (Inverewe Garden, Ross & Cromarty); 62-3 S & O Mathews (Merrie Cottage, Hampshire); 64 left Fritz von der Schulenburg/The Interior Archive; 64-5 Andrew Lawson (Westpark, Munich, Germany); 65 right Marianne Majerus (Bassibones); 66-7 S & O Mathews (Colwell Cottage, Isle Of Wight); 68-9 Richard Felber (East Hampton, Long Island);

69 below right Sunniva Harte (Frith Lodge, Mr & Mrs G. Cridland); 69 top right Marianne Majerus (Bassibones); 70-1 Jerry Harpur (Marguerite McBey, Tangier, Morocco); 72 below Andrew Lawson; 72 top S & O Mathews (Little Court, Hampshire); 73 Brigitte Perdereau; 74 J C Mayer - G Le Scanff; 75 Jacqui Hurst; 76-7 The Garden Picture Library (Brigitte Thomas); 76 left Jacqui Hurst (Kelly Castle, Fife); 77 right J C Mayer - G Le Scanff (Orne, France); 78-9 Jerry Harpur (Marguerite McBey, Tangier, Morocco); 79 right J C Mayer - G Le Scanff; 80 left Richard Felber (Michael Pollen, Cornwall, Connecticut); 80-1 Sunniva Harte (Wisley); 81 right Sunniva Harte (Wisley); 82 right Sunniva Harte (Geraldine Guest); 82 left Jacqui Hurst (Joy Larkham); 83 The Garden Picture Library (Juliette Wade); 84-5 The Garden Picture Library (Juliette Wade); 85-6 Juliette Wade (Sarah Sears & Carlo Jolly); 87 right Marianne Majerus (Ballymaloe Kitchen Garden); 88-9 Andrew Lawson (Flintham Hall, Nottinghamshire); 88 left S & O Mathews; 90-1 Jacqui Hurst; 90 left Howard Rice; 91 right Howard Rice; 92-3 The Garden Picture Library (Jerry Pavia); 93 right Sunniva Harte (Ethne Clarke, Sycamore Barn); 94 Juliette Wade (Jean & Peter Mathews, Yew Tree Cottage, Berkshire); 95 Brigitte Perdereau; 96 top Jacqui Hurst; 96 below John Glover (Gardeners Cottage, Cheshire); 97 Marianne Majerus (Felbrigg Hall); 98-9 Roger Foley (Colonial Williamsburg); 98 left Curtice Taylor (Stourton House Garden); 99 right S & O Mathews (Hightown Farm, Hampshire); 100 The Garden Picture Library (Ann Kelley); 100-1 Jacqui Hurst; 102 left Jacqui Hurst; 102-3 S & O Mathews; 103 right Marianne Majerus; 104-5 Richard Felber (Katherine Whiteside, Cold Springs, New York); 105 top Jacqui Hurst; 105 below Jacqui Hurst; 106 J C Mayer - G Le Scanff (Wy-Dit-Joli Village, France); 107 Jerry Harpur (Marguerite McBey, Tangier, Morocco); 108-9 Kari Haavisto (Salgkulla Farm, Owners: Sten & Kerstin Enbom; designer:Kerstin Enbom; architect: Sten Enbom); 109 right Andrew Lawson (Chilcombe House, Dorset); 110 below Marijke Heuff (Lenshoek, Holland); 110 top S & O Mathews (King John's Lodge, Sussex); 111 S & O Mathews (Little Court, Hampshire); 112-3 Marijke Heuff (Joseph Bayol, France); 114 below Roger Foley (Edelman Garden); 114-15 Sunniva Harte (Ethne Clark, Sycamore Barn); 115 right Sunniva Harte (Sunniva Harte, Lewes); 116 Jessie Walker (Burnham); 117 Richard Felber; 118 Jacqui Hurst (The Hall, Suffolk); 119 below Sunniva Harte (Frith Lodge, Mr & Mrs G. Cridland); 119 top Dency Kane (Anna Davis Garden, Atlanta); 120-1 Ken Druse; 121 right S & O Mathews (Park Farm, Essex); 122 left The Garden Picture Library (Marijke Heuff); 122-3 Sunniva Harte (Ethne Clarke, Sycamore Barn); 123 left The Garden Picture Library (Juliette Wade); 124-5 Gil Hanly (Sue Foster, Matongi Waikato); 124 left Juliette Wade (Mr & Mrs Vail, Upham, Hampshire); 126-7 The Garden Picture Library (Jane Legate); 127 right Neil Campbell-Sharp (Apple Court Nurseries, Hampshire); 128 Juliette Wade (Gwen Bishop, Combe, Oxon); 129 top Jerry Harpur (Ivan Hicks, Garden In Mind, Sussex); 129 below Andrew Lawson (Elton Hall, Cambridgeshire); 130-1 Marianne Majerus (Ballymaloe Kitchen Garden); 130 left Christian Sarramon; 131 right Andrew Lawson (Gothic House, Oxfordshire); 132-3 Marianne Majerus (Nun's Manor, Shepreth); 133 right Marianne Majerus (Woodpeckers, Warwickshire); 134-5 Jerry Harpur (Wesley & Susan Dixon, Lake Forest, Illinois, USA); 134 left Sunniva Harte (Sunniva Harte, Lewes); 135 right Juliette Wade (Jean & Peter Mathews, Yew Tree Cottage, Berkshire); 136-7 Andrew Lawson (Sutton Place, Surrey); 138 left Sunniva Harte (Brangwyn's House); 138-9 J C Mayer - G Le Scanff (Domaine de St Jean de Beauregard,France); 140 left J C Mayer - G Le Scanff (Jardin D'Andre Eve, France); 140-1 S & O Mathews (Park Farm, Essex); 141 right Inside/C. de Virieu.